VISUAL QUICKSTART GUIDE

FIREWORKS

FOR WINDOWS AND MACINTOSH

Sandee Cohen

Peachpit Press

macromedia®
PRESS

Visual QuickStart Guide

Fireworks for Windows and Macintosh

Sandee Cohen

Peachpit Press

1249 Eighth Street
Berkeley, CA 94710
510/524-2178
510/524-2221 (fax)
800/283-9444

Find us on the World Wide Web at:
http://www.peachpit.com
Published by Peachpit Press in association with Macromedia Press.
Peachpit Press is a division of Addison Wesley Longman

Copyright © 1998 by Sandee Cohen

Editor: Marjorie Baer
Production coordinator: Kate Reber
Copy editor: Nancy Dunn
Cover design: The Visual Group
Compositor: Sandee Cohen
Index: Steve Rath

This book was created using Fireworks for illustrations, QuarkXPress for layout, and Ambrosia SW Snapz Pro and Snagit for screen shots. The computers used were a Macintosh PowerPC™ 8500, a PowerBook 3400, and a Monorail 166LS. The fonts used were Minion Condensed and Futura Condensed from Adobe, and two specialty fonts created using Macromedia Fontographer.

Notice of Rights

Notice of Liability

Trademarks

ISBN 0-201-35361-X

9 8 7 6 5 4 3 2

Printed and bound in the United States of America

DEDICATED TO

My mom, Sylvia Cohen, who would have
wondered what is all the fuss about the Web.

My sister, Bonnie—and she knows why!

Terry—who thinks I work much too hard. (She
may be right.)

Dad, Jean, Jeffry, Dan, Elizabeth, and Sarah, who
should have learned something by now about
computer graphics.

THANKS TO

Nancy Ruenzel publisher of Peachpit Press.

Marjorie Baer my project editor at Peachpit Press who helped me structure the entire book.

Kate Reber of Peachpit Press who helped me with my first color pages.

The staff of Peachpit Press all of whom make me proud to be a Peachpit author.

Lynda Weinman who so graciously agreed to write the foreword. Lynda has been a pioneer in Web graphics. Our journey is much easier because she led the way. (www.lynda.com)

Nancy Dunn my copy editor who pretends not to understand what I write so I can be clearer.

Steve Rath who still does the best index in the business even though he moved.

Michael Greenberg who once again helped this print person understand details of the Web. (www.flashcentral.com)

David Mendels of Macromedia who first showed me Fireworks.

Tom Hale of Macromedia whose Fireworks demo helped me understand the program.

Diana Smedley of Macromedia who has been a lifeline of emergency assistance.

Doug Benson Macromedia who took time out from his busy schedule to answer my many e-mail questions.

David Morris of Macromedia who took a whole Saturday afternoon to explain it all to me.

Bentley Wolfe of Macromedia — simply the incomparable Bentley Wolfe.

Joanne Watkins of Macromedia who spent a weekend of her own time to tech edit the book as well as offer suggestions on content and copy.

Fireworks beta list too numerous to name, but who all gave me great insight into features and techniques.

Robert Farrell of Desktop America who created the artwork for the introduction of the book. (www. desktopamerica.com)

Robert Ransick and the staff of the New School for Social Research Computer Instruction Center.

Sharon Steuer author of the *Illustrator 7 Wow! Book* who helped me during more than one late-night panic attack.

Pixel my cat who thinks chapters 11 and 12 are all about her.

FOREWORD

When the World Wide Web first surfaced, no one ever imagined the popularity it would achieve. Since the text-based Internet existed long before the Web, it's safe to assume that graphics have played a huge role in the success the Web enjoys today.

Until now, there have been no dedicated programs that targeted creators of Web graphics. We have been forced to use many different products and utilities to accomplish the diverse number of graphics tasks required for Web development. Once you switch from whatever program(s) you're working with now, to a dedicated Web graphics editor, you are going to see a big boost in productivity and in the quality of your graphics.

Among the many great features Fireworks offers is the ability to work with editable text and artwork. This means that you or a client can easily make changes without starting over from scratch. The effects (which include embossing, glows, bevels, drop shadows, and much much more) will stay attached to the editable text, meaning that button creation has never been easier or more robust.

Since making buttons and navigation graphics is a huge part of your job as a Web designer, you might also want to include "rollover" graphics on your Web site (where the artwork changes when the end user touches it with his or her mouse). Before Fireworks, making rollover graphics normally required two steps: creating the graphics and writing the JavaScript code to enable the rollovers. Fireworks lets you focus on the design aspect of rollovers and buttons, since it will automatically produce the complex rollover JavaScript code for you!

You no longer need to leave your image editor to compress your images, since Fireworks has fantastic image-compression capabilities with handy previews to help you make informed decisions about which file format to use. Fireworks' ability to slice apart images can be used to mix and match file formats, or add animation/rollovers to a static image.

Fireworks is a deep and rich program that contains many innovations. Since it's a new breed of graphics editor though, it has a higher learning curve than a standard image editor. As I read Sandee Cohen's excellent *Fireworks Visual Quickstart Guide*, many hidden aspects of this program were revealed to me, as I am sure they will be revealed to you. This book delivers on its promise to get you up and running quickly, which is essential in the fast-paced world of Web development. I highly recommend this book if you want to use Fireworks to its best advantage.

Lynda Weinman

Author, *Designing Web Graphics.2*

http://www.lynda.com

TABLE OF CONTENTS

INTRODUCTION

Welcome to Macromedia Fireworks. Just like this book, Fireworks is totally new. The Fireworks application was released in the spring of 1998 in a public beta program. Then, after fixing bugs and adding several features, the first version was released a few months later. Ordinarily I write about software based on years of experience using the programs and teaching them to students. With Fireworks it has been exciting to learn the features and then write about them.

What you can create with Fireworks

Fireworks was specially designed to create graphics to be used on the World Wide Web. Before Fireworks, artists and designers used tools such as Adobe Photoshop, Illustrator, and Macromedia FreeHand that were originally created to produce print graphics. They then added other programs such as GIF Builder or DeBabelizer to convert the print graphics into Web formats. The process was very cumbersome, especially if there were any changes or edits to be made in the artwork. Fireworks gives you one tool that does it all, from start to finish. All your Web graphic elements—text, photos, buttons, banners, animations, and interface elements—can all be created, modified, optimized, and output from one Fireworks file. As the artwork at the end of this introduction shows, Fireworks has all the tools you need to create sophisticated graphics. This makes Fireworks a complete Web graphics solution.

How this book is organized

The first two chapters provide overviews of the program. The next dozen chapters cover all the tools and techniques for creating graphics from within Fireworks. This is where you learn to create artwork and add special effects. Chapter 15 covers exporting artwork out of Fireworks in various formats. Since exporting, converting file formats, and optimizing Web graphics are so important, you can easily start right away with that chapter. The final chapters cover advanced features such as rollovers and animations.

Using this book

If you have used any of the *Visual QuickStart Guides*, you will find this book very similar. Each of the chapters consists of numbered exercises that deal with a specific technique or feature of the program. As you work through each exercise, you gain an understanding of the technique or feature. The illustrations for each of the exercises help you judge if you are following the steps correctly.

Instructions

Using a book such as this, you will find works better once you understand the terms I am using. This is especially important since some other computer books use terms differently. Therefore, here are the terms I use in the book and explanations of what they mean.

Click refers to pressing down and releasing the mouse button on the Macintosh, or the left mouse button on Windows. You must release the mouse button or it is not a click. *Press* means to hold down the mouse button, or the keyboard key.

Press and drag means to hold the mouse button down and then move the mouse. In later chapters, I use the shorthand term *drag;* just remember that you have to press and hold as you drag the mouse.

Menu commands

Fireworks has menu commands that you follow to open dialog boxes, change artwork, and invoke certain commands. These menu commands are listed in bold type. The typical direction to choose a menu command might be written as **Modify > Arrange > Bring to Front**. This means that you should first choose the Modify menu, then choose the Arrange submenu, and then choose the Bring to Front command.

Keyboard shortcuts

Most of the menu commands for Fireworks have keyboard shortcuts that help you work faster. For instance, instead of choosing New from the File menu, it is faster and easier to use the keyboard shortcut.

The modifier keys useds in keyboard short-cuts are sometimes listed in different orders by different software companies or authors. For example I always list the Command or Ctrl keys first, then the Option or Alt key, and then the Shift key. Other people may list the Shift key first. The order that you press those modifier keys is not important. However, it is very important that you always add the last key (the letter or number key) after you are holding the other keys.

The keyboard shortcuts for the menu commands are listed in Appendix B. There are several reasons for not including those shortcuts right in the book. Most importantly, many of the keyboard shortcuts for the Macintosh platform differ from those for the Windows platform. This means that the shortcut for **File > Save As** would have appeared in the text as Command-Shift-S/ Ctrl-Shift-S. Rather than clutter the exercises, they are listed in Appendix B separated by platform.

Learning keyboard shortcuts

While keyboard shortcuts help you work faster, you really do not have to start using them right away. In fact, you will most likely learn more about Fireworks by using the menus. As you look for one command, you may see another feature that you would like to explore.

Once you feel comfortable working with Fireworks, you can start adding keyboard shortcuts to your repertoire. My suggestion is to look at which menu commands you use a lot. Then each day choose one of those shortcuts. For instance, if you import a lot of art from other programs, you might decide to learn the shortcut for the Import command. For the rest of that day use the Import shortcut every time you import art. Even if you have to look at the menu to refresh your memory, still use the keyboard shortcut to actually open the

Import dialog box. By the end of the day you will have memorized the Import shortcut. The next day you can learn a new one.

Cross-platform issues

One of the great strengths of Fireworks is that it is almost identical on both the Macintosh and Windows platforms. In fact, at first glance it is hard to tell which platform you are working on. However, because there are some differences between the platforms, there are some things you should keep in mind.

Modifier keys

Modifier keys are always listed with the Macintosh key first and then the Windows key second. So a direction to hold the Command/Ctrl key as you drag means to hold the Command key on the Macintosh platform or the Ctrl key on the Windows platform. When the key is the same on both computers, such as the Shift key, only one key is listed.

Generally the Command key on the Macintosh (sometimes called the Apple key) corresponds to the Ctrl key on Windows. The Option key on the Macintosh corresponds to the Alt key on Windows. The Control key on the Macintosh does not have an equivalent on Windows. Notice that the Control key for the Macintosh is always spelled out while the Ctrl key for Windows is not.

Platform-specific features

A few times in the book, I have written separate exercises for the Macintosh and Windows platforms. These exercises are indicated by (Mac) and (Win).

Most of the time this is because the procedures are so different that they need to be written separately. Some features exist only on one platform. Those features are then labeled as to their platform.

Interface features

Most of the illustrations of the interface were taken on my Macintosh computer and cropped so that the platform is not too obvious. When necessary, I have put both the Macintosh and Windows elements on one page.

Learning Fireworks

If you have been working with Web graphics for some time, then all you need to do is learn the specific features of Fireworks. However, if you are new to the Web, you may need some background information on Web graphics. I have tried to provide some in each of the Fireworks chapters. You may want to read some additional material. Some of the books I like are *Designing Web Graphics.2* by Lynda Weinman, and *The Non-Designer's Web Book* by Robin Williams and John Tollett.

And remember to have fun!

Sandee Cohen (SandeeC@aol.com)
June 1998

©R. Farrell, 1998

An example of the many differnt types of artwork effects you can create using Fireworks. (Artwork courtesy of Robert Farrell of Desktop America Training, NYC)

FIREWORKS BASICS 1

Before you can start working with Fireworks, there are a few preliminary things you need to cover. For instance, you should be familiar with the controls in the document window and the names of the onscreen elements. This way you will be able to quickly find the correct panels in the later chapters.

In this chapter you will learn

The system requirements.

The way to install Fireworks.

The way to launch Fireworks.

The elements of the Layers panel.

The elements of the Frame panel.

The elements of the Brush panel.

The elements of the Fill panel.

The elements of the Effect panel.

The elements of the Swatches panel.

The elements of the Color Mixer.

The elements of the Tool Options panel.

The elements of the Text Editor.

The elements and keyboard shortcuts of the Toolbox.

The elements of the Main toolbar.

The elements of the Modify toolbar.

The elements of the Info bar.

The elements of the Object toolbar.

The elements of the URL toolbar.

The elements of the View Controls toolbar.

The way to work with the interface elements.

The way to work with the pop-up slider controls.

System Requirements (Mac)

You can find out how much memory you have by choosing About This Computer from the Apple menu ❶. You can find out how much hard disk space you have by opening the hard disk and reading the available space at the top of the window ❷.

The minimum system required to run Fireworks:

- System 7.5.5 or higher
- Adobe Type Manager 4 or higher to use Type 1 fonts
- Power Macintosh processor required (Power Macintosh 604/120 MHz or greater, 603e/180 MHz or greater, or G3 recommended)
- 24 MB of application RAM with virtual memory on (32 MB or more with virtual memory off recommended)
- 60 MB of available hard disk space (100 MB or more recommended)
- CD-ROM drive
- Mouse or digitizing tablet
- 640×480 resolution, 256-color monitor required (1024×768 resolution, millions-of-colors monitor recommended)

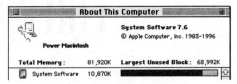

❶ *The Macintosh* **Memory** *display*

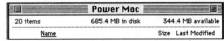

❷ *The Macintosh* **Hard Disk** space *display*

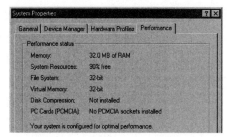

❸ *The Windows* **System Properties** *display*

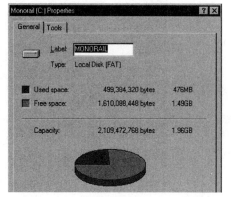

❹ *The Windows* **Hard Disk Properties** *display*

System Requirements (Win)

You can find out how much memory you have by choosing System from the Control Panels directory ❸. You can find out how much hard disk space you have by selecting the hard disk, and clicking with the right mouse button, and then choosing Properties from the contextual menu ❹.

The minimum system required to run Fireworks:

- Windows 95 or Windows NT 4 (with Service Pack 3) or later

- Intel Pentium 120 MHz processor required (Pentium 166 MHz with MMX recommended)

- 32 MB of system RAM on Windows 95 (40 MB or more recommended on Windows NT)

- 60 MB of available hard disk space (100 MB or more recommended)

- CD-ROM drive

- Mouse or digitizing tablet

- 640×480 resolution, 256-color monitor required (1024×768 resolution, millions-ofolors monitor recommended)

Once you have confirmed that your system meets the minimum requirements for running Fireworks, you can then install the application.

To install Fireworks (Mac)

1. Disable any virus-protection software.
2. Insert the Fireworks CD-ROM in the CD-ROM drive.
3. Double-click the Fireworks installer ❺.
4. Follow the instructions that appear.
5. After installation, restart the Macintosh.

To install Fireworks (Win)

1. Insert the Fireworks CD-ROM in the CD-ROM drive.
2. Follow the instructions that appear ❻.
3. After installation, restart the computer.

Once you have installed Fireworks, you can then launch the application.

To launch Fireworks (Mac)

Open the folder that contains the Fireworks application and then double-click the Fireworks application icon ❼.

To launch Fireworks (Win)

Use the Start menu ❽ to navigate to the Fireworks folder and then choose the Fireworks application.

Fireworks Installer

❺ *The* **Fireworks installer** *for the Macintosh*

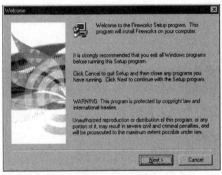

❻ *The opening screen for the Fireworks installer for Windows*

Fireworks

❼ *The Fireworks application icon*

❽ *The Fireworks application in the Start menu*

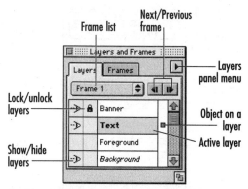

Frame list

Next/Previous frame

Layers panel menu

Lock/unlock layers

Object on a layer

Active layer

Show/hide layers

❾ *The elements of the* **Layers panel**

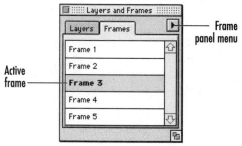

Frame panel menu

Active frame

❿ *The elements of the* **Frames panel**

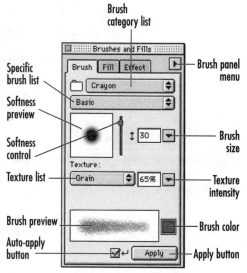

Brush category list

Specific brush list

Softness preview

Softness control

Texture list

Brush preview

Auto-apply button

Brush panel menu

Brush size

Texture intensity

Brush color

Apply button

⓫ *The elements of the* **Brush panel**

Once you have launched Fireworks, you see the various Fireworks onscreen elements. The different toolbars, panels, and window elements allow you to create Fireworks graphics. These elements can be closed, opened, resized, or rearranged to suit your own work habits.

The Layers and Frames panels appear as one unit. Click the tab for either the Layers or Frames panel to work with those particular features.

Elements of the Layers panel

The Layers panel ❾ allows you to control the order in which objects appear onscreen. (*For more information on the Layers panel, see Chapter 6, "Working With Objects."*)

Elements of the Frames panel

The Frames panel ❿ controls the elements used for creating animations. (*For more information on the Frames panel, see Chapter 19, "Animations."*)

The Brush, Fill, and Effect panels appear as one unit. Click the tab for a panel to work with its features.

Elements of the Brush panel

The Brush panel ⓫ controls the look of the brush effect, or brush stroke, that is applied to the edge of an object. (*For more information on brushes, see Chapter 8, "Brushes."*)

Layers Panel; Frames Panel; Brush Panel

Elements of the Fill panel

The Fill panel ⓬ controls the effect that is applied to the area inside an object. (*For more information on working with fills, see Chapter 7, "Fills."*)

Elements of the Effect panel

The Effect panel ⓭ controls the additional effects that can be added to an object. (*For more information on Effects, see Chapter 9, "Effects."*)

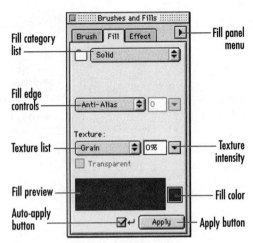

Fill category list — — Fill panel menu

Fill edge controls —

Texture list — — Texture intensity

Fill preview — — Fill color

Auto-apply button — — Apply button

⓬ *The elements of the* Fill panel

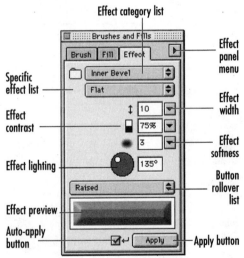

Effect category list

Specific effect list — — Effect panel menu

Effect contrast — — Effect width

Effect lighting — — Effect softness

Effect preview — — Button rollover list

Auto-apply button — — Apply button

⓭ *The elements of the* Effect panel

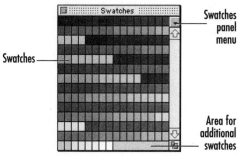

Swatches

Swatches panel menu

Area for additional swatches

⓮ *The elements of the* **Swatches panel** *as a floating panel*

Elements of the Swatches panel

The Swatches panel **⓮** lets you work with preset palettes of color or store your own sets of colors. In the Windows version of Fireworks, the Swatches panel can be fixed to the side of the application window **⓯** or positioned as a floating panel. (*For more information on the color modes, see Chapter 3, "Colors."*)

Elements of the Color Mixer

The Color Mixer **⓰** allows you to define colors according to five different modes: RGB, Hexadecimal, HSB, CMY, or Grayscale. (*For more information on the color modes, see Chapter 3, "Colors."*)

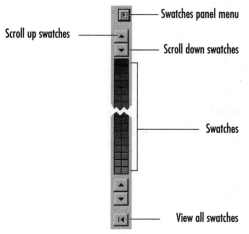

Swatches panel menu

Scroll up swatches

Scroll down swatches

Swatches

View all swatches

⓯ *The elements of the* **Swatches panel** *as part of the application window (Win)*

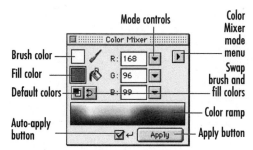

Mode controls

Color Mixer mode menu

Brush color

Fill color

Default colors

Swap brush and fill colors

Color ramp

Auto-apply button

Apply button

⓰ *The elements of the* **Color Mixer**

Elements of the Tool Options panel

The Tool Options panel ⑰ displays any options for working with the currently selected tool. These options change depending on the tool selected.

⑰ *The elements of the* Tool Options *panel*

Elements of the Text Editor

The Text Editor ⑱ lets you enter and format text. (*For more information on working with text, see Chapter 10, "Text."*)

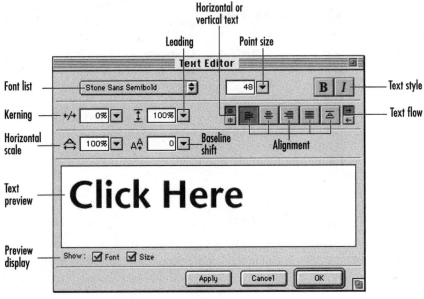

⑱ *The elements of the* Text Editor

Elements and keyboard shortcuts of the Toolbox

Fireworks has 32 different tools. You can choose the tools by clicking the tool in the Toolbox ⑲ or by pressing the pop-up group.

You can also access the tools by pressing the keyboard shortcut (shown in parenthesis) for each tool. Unlike other actions, the tool shortcuts do not need modifiers keys such as Command or Ctrl.

TIP In the Windows version of Fireworks, the Toolbox can be fixed to the side of the application window or positioned as a floating panel.

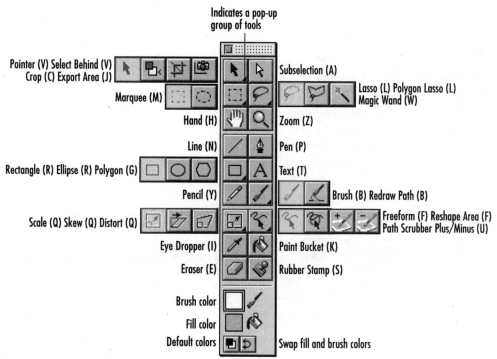

Indicates a pop-up group of tools

Pointer (V) Select Behind (V) Crop (C) Export Area (J)

Subselection (A)

Marquee (M)

Lasso (L) Polygon Lasso (L) Magic Wand (W)

Hand (H)

Zoom (Z)

Line (N)

Pen (P)

Rectangle (R) Ellipse (R) Polygon (G)

Text (T)

Pencil (Y)

Brush (B) Redraw Path (B)

Scale (Q) Skew (Q) Distort (Q)

Freeform (F) Reshape Area (F) Path Scrubber Plus/Minus (U)

Eye Dropper (I)

Paint Bucket (K)

Eraser (E)

Rubber Stamp (S)

Brush color

Fill color

Default colors

Swap fill and brush colors

⑲ *The tools in the **Toolbox** and their keyboard shortcuts (in parentheses)*

Toolbox

Elements of the Main toolbar (Win)

The Main toolbar ❷⓿ gives you easy access to the most commonly used commands. The Main toolbar can be fixed to the sides of the application window or positioned as a floating panel.

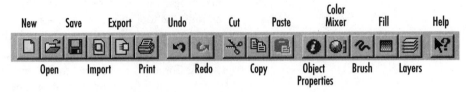

❷⓿ *The elements of the* **Main toolbar**

Elements of the Modify toolbar (Win)

The Modify toolbar ❷❶ provides easy access to the most commonly used modification commands. The Modify toolbar can be fixed to the sides of the application window or positioned as a floating panel.

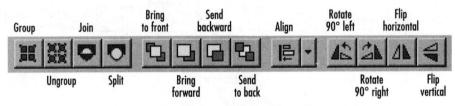

❷❶ *The elements of the* **Modify toolbar**

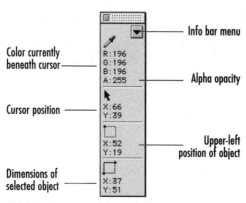

Color currently beneath cursor

Cursor position

Dimensions of selected object

Info bar menu

Alpha opacity

Upper-left position of object

㉒ *The elements of the* Info bar

Elements of the Info bar

The Info bar **㉒** provides feedback as to the color and position of selected objects. In the Windows version of Fireworks, the Info bar can be fixed to the side of the application window or positioned as a floating panel. (*For more information on using the Info bar, see page 40.*)

Elements of the Object toolbar

The Object toolbar **㉓** controls the opacity of objects and how they interact with other objects on the page. In the Windows version of Fireworks, the Object toolbar can be fixed to the edge of the application window or positioned as a floating panel. (*For more information on using the Object toolbar, see pages 89 and 92.*)

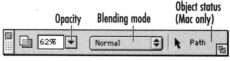

Opacity   Blending mode   Object status (Mac only)

㉓ *The elements of the* Object toolbar

Elements of the URL toolbar

The URL toolbar **㉔** allows you to add URL links to areas on the page. In the Windows version of Fireworks, the URL toolbar can be fixed to the edge of the application window or positioned as a floating panel. (*For more information on adding links to areas of your Web graphics, see Chapter 16, "Image Maps" and Chapter 17, "Slices."*)

Show/Hide URL layer   Create URL shapes   Assign URLs

URL pointer   Slice object tool

URLs menu

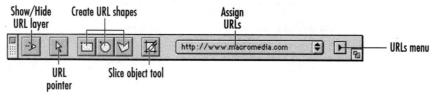

㉔ *The elements of the* URL toolbar

Info Bar; Object Toolbar; URL toolbar

Elements of the View Controls toolbar

The View Controls toolbar **25** is part of the document window. It lets you change the magnification and display of your page. In the Windows version of Fireworks, the View Controls toolbar **26** can be fixed to the edge of the application window or positioned as a floating panel. (*For more information on using the View Controls toolbar, see page 27.*)

Magnification Display Page Preview

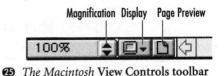

25 *The Macintosh* View Controls toolbar

Working with the interface elements

You set many of the Fireworks features using panels and dialog boxes. Though the panels and dialog boxes differ in function and layout, they all use similar interface devices that you adjust to control the settings **27**.

Magnification   Display Page Preview

26 *The Windows* View Controls toolbar

View Controls Toolbar; Interface Elements

Click a tab   Click a box   Press to open a pop-up menu

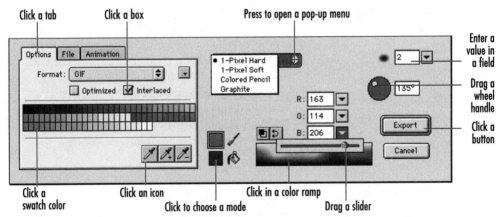

27 *A composite dialog box that shows the* interface elements *and how you control them.*

28 *Slider controls in the closed positions*

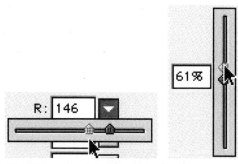

29 *Slider controls being manipulated*

Working with pop-up sliders:

Most elements of the Fireworks interface will look familiar to you if you have used a Mac or Windows program before. One interface element is fairly new to graphics applications: the pop-up slider. It is a slider control that does not look like a slider control at first glance. When closed, such as in the R, G, B, controls, or in the Brush, Fill, and Effect panels **28**, the slider collapses into a small triangle control.

You can set those controls by typing in the field, but you can also press the triangle to reveal the slider control **29**. Then drag the small pointer to change the amount in the field. When you release the mouse button, the slider collapses and the amount is entered in the field.

DOCUMENT SETUP 2

Once you have launched Fireworks, you can begin work. You can start by creating a new Fireworks document or you can open an existing document. You can also open scanned images from other programs. Once you have a document open, there are various controls that affect how the document is displayed and how you work in the document.

In this chapter you will learn how to

Open a new document.

Set the canvas size.

Set the resolution.

Set the canvas color.

Change the canvas size.

Change the canvas color.

Open existing documents as untitled.

Display the document rulers.

Change the zero point.

Create guides.

Edit guides.

View the document grid.

Edit the document grid.

Use the magnification commands.

Use the Zoom tool.

Change the display options.

When you start a new document, you must make certain decisions about the document that affect the final output.

To create a new document:

1. Choose **File > New**. This opens the New Document dialog box **❶**.

2. Use the height and width fields to set the size of the document.

TIP Use the pop-up list to change the unit of measurement from pixels to inches or centimeters.

3. Use the resolution field to set the number of points per inch or the detail of the document.

TIP Most Web graphics are saved at 72 pixels per inch. Print graphics usually need higher resolutions.

TIP Once the document's resolution has been set, it cannot be changed.

4. Set the canvas color, or the color of the backmost layer of the document, by choosing white, transparent, or custom.

5. If you choose custom, click the small color box to open the color picker, where you can set your color.

6. Click OK to create the new document which appears in an untitled document window **❷**.

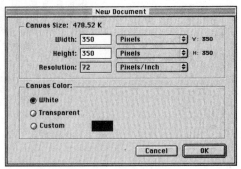

❶ *The* **New Document** *dialog box*

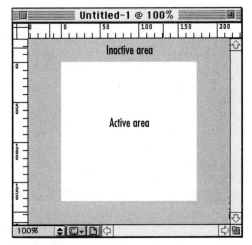

❷ *The* **document window**

New Document

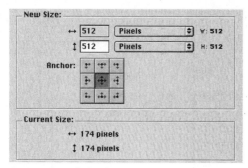

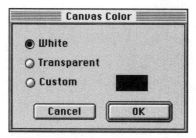

❸ New size *dialog box*

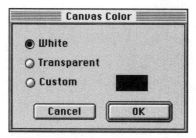

❹ *The* Canvas Color *dialog box*

Once you have created a document, you can still change its size and color.

To change the canvas size:

1. Choose **Modify** > **Document** > **Canvas Size** to open the Canvas Size dialog box ❸.

2. Use the New Size height and width fields.

TIP Use the Current Size information as a reference.

3. Click the anchor area to determine where the canvas will be added to or subtracted from.

4. Click OK to apply the changes to your document.

TIP If you reduce the size of your document, objects in the clipped areas are not lost. Although they are not visible, you can move them back into the active area where they reappear.

To change the canvas color:

1. Choose **Modify** > **Document** > **Canvas Color** to open the Canvas Color dialog box ❹.

2. Click white, transparent, or custom.

3. If you choose custom, click the color square to open the color picker to choose a specific color.

Canvas Size; Canvas Color

You may want to make changes to a document without losing the original version. Fireworks lets you protect the original file by opening it as an untitled document.

To open a document as untitled:

1. Choose **File**>**Open** and navigate to find the original version of the file.

2. Click Open as "Untitled" and then click Open. The document opens in an unsaved, untitled version.

3. Make any changes and save the document as you would any other file.

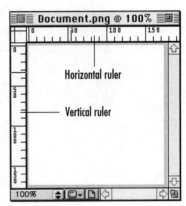

❺ *The* **rulers** *in the document window*

If you want to work more precisely in your document, you will need to work with the rulers.

To display the document rulers:

Choose **View**>**Rulers**. The rulers appear at the top and left sides of the document **❺**. The rulers are displayed in the unit of pixels.

TIP Two lines appear on the rulers that track your position as you move around the document.

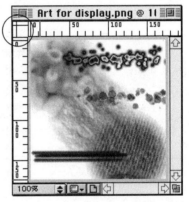

❻ Drag the zero-point crosshairs *(circled) onto the page to set the new zero point.*

Fireworks uses the upper-left corner of a document as its *zero point*, or the point where the rulers start. You can change the zero point for a document. This can help you position items on the page.

To change the zero point:

1. Drag the zero-point crosshairs onto the page **❻**.

2. Double-click the zero-point crosshairs in the corner of the document window to reset the zero point to the upper-left corner.

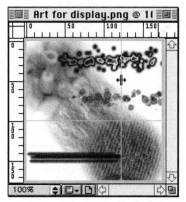

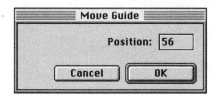

❼ **Dragging a guide** *from the ruler onto the active area*

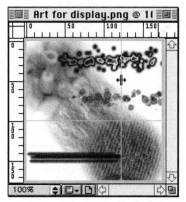

❽ *The* **Move Guide** *dialog box*

The rulers also let you add guides that you can use to align objects.

To create guides:

1. Drag from the left ruler to create a vertical guide ❼. Release the mouse button to place the guide.

2. Drag from the top ruler to create a horizontal guide. Release the mouse button to place the guide.

3. Repeat to add as many horizontal or vertical guides as you need.

To position guides:

Drag an existing guide to move it to a new position.

or

Double-click the guide to open the Move Guide dialog box ❽ and enter the exact position of the guide.

TIP Use **View** > **Snap To Guides** to have objects automatically snap, or align, to the guides.

Create Guides; Position Guides

There are several ways you can edit or control the look of guides.

To edit guides:

1. Choose **View>Edit Guides** to open the Grids and Guides dialog box ❾.

2. Click the color box to open the color picker and choose a new color to make the guides look more or less obvious.

3. Click Show Guides to show or hide the guides.

4. Click Snap to Guides to turn on or off the snap-to-guides feature.

5. Click Lock Guides to keep the guides from being moved.

TIP You can also lock the guides by choosing **View>Lock Guides**.

6. Click Clear All to delete all the guides from the document.

7. Click OK to apply the changes.

TIP Click the Grid tab to switch from editing the guides to editing the grid (*see next exercise*).

❾ *The* **Grids and Guides** *dialog box in the Guides mode*

In addition to guides, Fireworks has a grid, which you can use to align objects.

To view the document grid:

Choose **View>Grid** to display the document grid ❿. You can use the document grid to arrange your images into certain areas or to make sure objects are aligned or have the same size.

TIP You can use **View>Snap to Grid** to have objects automatically snap, or align, to the grid.

TIP When Snap to Grid is turned on, objects snap to the grid even if the grid is not visible.

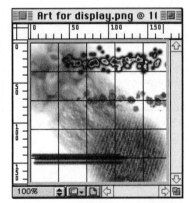

❿ *The* **document grid** *shown over the art*

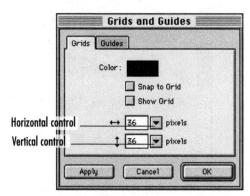

⑪ *The* **Grids and Guides** *dialog box in the Grid mode*

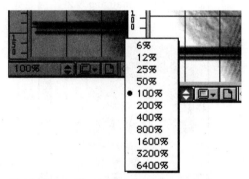

⑫ *The* **Magnification control menu** *at the bottom of the document window*

You can also change the size of the grid. This makes it easy to create objects all the same size or shape.

To edit the document grid:

1. Choose **View** > **Edit Grid** to open the Grids and Guides dialog box **⑪**.

2. Click the color box to open the color picker and choose a new color for the grid.

3. Press the horizontal control to open the slider or type in the field to increase or decrease the horizontal spacing.

4. Press the vertical control to open the slider or type in the field to increase or decrease the vertical spacing.

5. Click Snap to Grid to turn on or off the snap-to-grid feature.

6. Click Show Grid to show or hide the document grid.

You may need to zoom in or out to see specific areas or the big picture.

To use the magnification commands:

To zoom to a specific magnification, use the magnification control **⑫**.

or

Choose **View** > **Magnification** and then choose a specific magnification.

or

Choose **View** > **Zoom In** or **View** > **Zoom Out** to jump to a specific magnification.

or

Choose **View** > **Fit Selection** to display the object selected.

or

Choose **View** > **Fit All** to display the entire document.

You can use the Zoom tool to jump to a specific magnification and position.

To use the Zoom tool:

1. Click the Zoom tool in the Toolbox.

2. Click the Zoom tool on the area you want to zoom in on. Click as many times as you need to get as close as necessary to the area you want to see.

   or

   Drag the Zoom tool diagonally across the area you want to see. Release the mouse button to zoom in **⓫–⓬**.

   TIP Press Command/Ctrl and Spacebar to access the Zoom tool without leaving the tool that is currently selected.

   TIP Press the Option/Alt key while in the Zoom tool to zoom out from objects. The icon changes from a plus sign (+) to a minus sign (−).

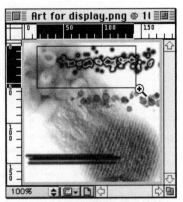

⓫ *Use the* **Zoom tool** *to zoom in on a specific area by dragging a marquee around that area. The line indicates the area being selected.*

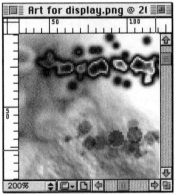

⓬ *After dragging, the selected area fills the window.*

Zoom Tool

Display mode
control

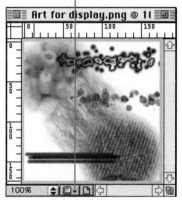

⓯ *The* **Full Display** *mode shows all the fills, brushes, and effects for the objects.*

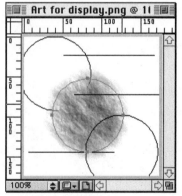

⓰ *The* **Draft Display** *mode shows only the paths for the unselected objects. The selected object shows its fills, brushes, or effects.*

Fireworks lets you work in two different display modes. The Full Display mode **⓯** shows all the objects in the document with their fills, brushes, and effects.

The Draft Display mode **⓰** shows only the paths for all the unselected objects. Only the selected object displays its fill, brush, or effect.

To change the display options:

1. Press the Display mode control at the bottom of the document window.

2. Choose between Full Display or Draft Display.

   or

   Choose **View > Full Display** or **View > Draft Display** to change the display mode.

Display Options

COLORS 3

S ince Fireworks was developed to create graphics for display on the World Wide Web, it has special features for working with colors on the Web. This means you can create graphics that do not shift color when viewed by different Web browsers. However, you are not limited to just Web colors. Fireworks also lets you define colors using several other color systems.

In this chapter you will learn how to

Use the Color Mixer.

Define RGB colors.

Define hexadecimal colors.

Define CMY colors.

Define HSB colors.

Define Grayscale colors.

Use the Swatches panel.

Choose the Web 216 palette swatches.

Choose the Macintosh System swatches.

Choose the Windows System swatches.

Choose the Grayscale swatches.

Add colors to the Swatches panel.

Delete colors from the Swatches panel.

Save colors in the Swatches panel.

Load colors to the Swatches panel.

Sort the swatches by color.

Use the default colors.

Use the Eyedropper to sample colors.

Use the Paint Bucket to fill colors.

Use the Info bar color information.

Two panels control color in Fireworks. The first, the Color Mixer, lets you to define your own colors to use in your document.

To use the Color Mixer:

1. If you do not see the Color Mixer, choose **Window>Color Mixer**.

   or

   Click the title bar of the Color Mixer panel to bring it in front of any other onscreen elements.

2. Use the Mode menu to choose from the five different color modes **❶**.

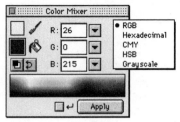

❶ *The* **five color mode choices** *of the Color Mixer*

Because the Web is viewed on computer monitors or television screens, one of the most common ways of defining colors for Web graphics is to use the RGB (Red, Green, Blue) color system, also called *additive* color. This is the system used in computer monitors. (*See the color insert for a diagram of how additive colors can be mixed.*) In the additive color system, all three colors combine into white. Each of the RGB components is given a number between 0 and 255. So a yellow color could have the RGB values of R: 250, G: 243, and B: 117.

To define RGB colors:

1. Make sure the Color Mixer mode is set to RGB.

2. To choose the R (Red) component, drag the slider or enter a value in the R field **❷**. Do the same for the G (Green) component and the B (Blue) component.

   or

   Click anywhere along the RGB color ramp at the bottom of the Color Mixer to choose colors by eye, rather than by numeric values.

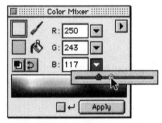

❷ Drag the slider *to set the value for one of the RGB color components. The RGB colors are set with numbers from 0 to 255.*

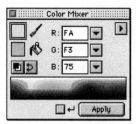

❸ **Hexadecimal colors** *use combinations of letters and numbers to define colors.*

Text, links, and background colors of Web graphics are defined for the Web by using a color system called *hexadecimal*. Instead of numbers from 0 to 255, the hexadecimal system uses combinations of letters and numbers. So the yellow in the previous exercise would be defined in hexadecimal as R: FA, G: F3, B: 75.

To define hexadecimal colors:

1. Make sure the Color Mixer mode is set to Hexadecimal.

2. To choose the R (red) component, drag the slider or enter a value in the R field ❸. Do the same for the G (green) component or the B (blue) component.

or

Click in the color ramp at the bottom of the Color Mixer to choose colors by eye, rather than by numbers.

TIP The color ramp in the hexadecimal mode limits you to working with the 216 Web-safe colors (*see page 35*).

TIP The hexadecimal system uses one or two-digit combinations of the following characters: 0, 1, 2, 3, 4, 5, 6, 7, 8, 9, A, B, C, D, E, F. Other characters are ignored.

TIP You can also use the hexadecimal codes from your Fireworks graphics as part of the HTML code for your Web pages.

For more information on hexadecimal codes, see *HTML For the World Wide Web Visual QuickStart Guide* by Elizabeth Castro or *The Non-Designer's Web Book* by Robin Williams and John Tollett, both published by Peachpit Press, or see *Coloring Web Graphics.2* by Lynda Weinman published by New Riders Publishing.

Hexadecimal Colors

You can also define colors using pure CMY, or cyan, magenta, and yellow colors. This is a *subtractive* color system in which all three colors combine to create black. (*See the color insert for a diagram of how subtractive colors can be mixed.*) Like the RGB system, the CMY components are defined using numbers from 0 to 255. If you have worked primarily in print, you may find it easier to mix colors using the CMY mode.

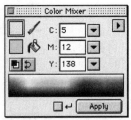

➍ **CMY colors** *use the numbers from 0 to 255 to set the amount of each color component to define colors.*

To define CMY colors:

1. Make sure the Color Mixer mode is set to CMY.

2. To choose the C (cyan) component, drag the slider or enter a value in the C field ➍. Do the same for the M (magenta) component or the Y (yellow) component.

   or

   Click anywhere along the CMY color ramp at the bottom of the Color Mixer to choose colors by eye, rather than by numeric values.

TIP The pure CMY colors are not the same as the CMYK colors used in printing. Theoretically (and in Fireworks), combining the three pure CMY colors produces black. In actual printing, combining the three CMY inks produces a muddy brown-black. So an extra black printing plate is added to create real black.

CMY Colors

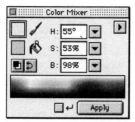

❺ **HSB colors** *use a combination of degrees around the color wheel for hue and percentages of saturation and brightness to define colors.*

You can also define colors using the classic HSB or Hue, Saturation, and Brightness system. Hue uses the principle of arranging colors in a wheel. Changing the colors from 0 to 360° moves through the entire color spectrum. Saturation uses percentage values, where 100% is a totally saturated color. Lower saturation values create pastel vesions of a color. Brightness uses percentage values where 100% is a color with no darkness or black. The lower the brightness percentage the more darkness or black is added to the color.

To define HSB colors:

1. Make sure the Color Mixer mode is set to HSB.

2. To choose the hue (H) component, drag the slider or enter a degree value in the H field ❺.

3. To choose the saturation (S) component, drag the slider or enter a percentage value in the S field. Do the same for the brightness (B) component.

   or

   Click anywhere along the HSB color ramp at the bottom of the Color Mixer to choose colors by eye, rather than by numeric values.

While Fireworks graphics are exported in RGB or indexed colors, you may need to match colors used in grayscale images. So the Color Mixer also lets you define colors using values of a single black (K) color plate.

To define Grayscale colors:

1. Make sure the Color Mixer mode is set to Grayscale.

2. To choose the black (K) component, drag the slider or enter a value in the K field ❻.

   or

   Click anywhere along the grayscale color ramp at the bottom of the Color Mixer to choose colors by eye, rather than by numeric values.

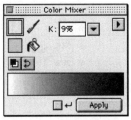

❻ **Grayscale colors** *use percentages of black to define colors.*

The second panel for working with colors is the Swatches panel. The Swatches panel lets you access preset palettes of swatches.

To use the Swatches panel:

1. If you do not see the Swatches panel, choose **Window>Swatches panel.**

   or

   If the Swatches panel is behind another panel, click the title bar of the Swatches panel to bring it in front of any other onscreen elements.

2. Use the Swatches panel menu to access the Swatches commands ❼.

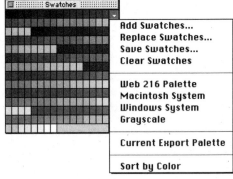

❼ *The* **Swatches panel menu**

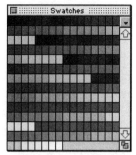

❽ *The* 216 Web-safe colors *in the Swatches panel (See the color insert for the color version of this illustration.)*

One of the most important considerations in creating Web graphics is using *Web-safe colors*. Web-safe colors are those colors that can be displayed predictably by different Web browsers as well as different computer systems. There are 216 Web-safe colors. Limiting your Fireworks graphics to only those 216 colors ensures that the colors of your document do not shift unexpectedly when they are displayed by different monitors using different browsers. You access the 216 Web-safe colors via the Swatches panel.

To choose the Web 216 palette swatches:

Open the Swatches panel menu and choose Web 216 Palette. The color swatches appear in the panel **❽**.

You can also limit your colors to the colors found in the Macintosh operating system. To do so, you can choose the Macintosh System colors.

To choose the Macintosh System swatches:

Open the Swatches panel menu and choose Macintosh System. The 256 color swatches appear in the area of the panel **❾**.

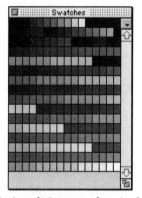

❾ *The* Macintosh System colors *in the Swatches panel (See the color insert for the color version of this illustration.)*

Just as you can pick colors using the Macintosh system colors, you can also pick colors using the Windows System colors.

To choose the Windows System swatches:

Open the Swatches panel menu and choose Windows System. The 256 color swatches appear in the panel ❿.

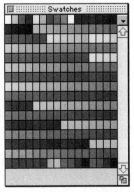

❿ *The* **Windows System colors** *in the Swatches panel (See the color insert for the color version of this illustration.)*

You can also limit your colors to grayscale colors. This is done by choosing the Grayscale swatches.

To choose the Grayscale swatches:

Open the Swatches panel menu and choose Grayscale. The 256 grayscale color swatches appear in the panel ⓫.

You can also use the Swatches panel to store colors that you create in the Color Mixer. This makes it easy to maintain a consistent look in all your graphics.

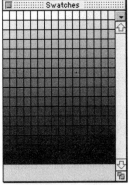

⓫ *The* **Grayscale colors** *in the Swatches panel*

To add colors to the Swatches panel:

1. Use the Color Mixer to define a color that you want to store.

2. Move the mouse over to the gray area at the bottom of the Swatches panel where there are no swatches. A paint bucket cursor appears ⓬.

3. Click the mouse button. The new color appears in its own color swatch.

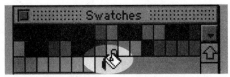

⓬ *The* **paint bucket cursor** *indicates you can store a color in the Swatches panel.*

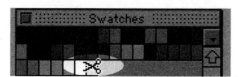

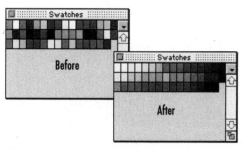

⓭ *The Command/Ctrl key displays the* **scissors cursor** *which allows you to delete a color from the Swatches panel.*

⓮ *The Swatches panel before and after* **sorting** the colors

You can also delete colors from the Swatches panel.

To delete colors from the Swatches panel:

1. Move the mouse over the swatch for the color you want to delete.

2. Hold the Command/Ctrl key. A scissors cursor appears ⓭.

3. Click the mouse button to delete the color from the Swatches panel.

You can also delete all the colors from the Swatches panel at once.

To delete all the colors from the Swatches panel:

Choose Clear Swatches from the Swatches panel menu.

If you keep adding colors to the Swatches panel, you may want to arrange the swatches so that similar colors are grouped together. To do so, you use the Sort by Color command.

To sort the swatches by color:

Choose Sort by Color from the Swatches panel menu. The various color swatches in the panel are automatically sorted, first by hue and then from light to dark ⓮.

Once you have created a custom Swatches panel with your own colors, you can save that Swatches panel to use at other times.

To save colors in the Swatches panel:

1. Choose Save Swatches from the Swatches panel menu.

2. Give the file a name and then save the file. This file can then be loaded into the Swatches panel.

To load colors to the Swatches panel:

Choose Replace Swatches from the Swatches panel menu. Then open a previously saved Swatches panel file. This replaces the current set of swatches with those from the saved file.

or

Choose Add Swatches from the Swatches panel menu. Then open a previously saved Swatches panel file. This adds the new swatches to those already in the Swatches panel.

TIP The Fireworks Swatches panel can also load swatches created in Adobe Photoshop.

Fireworks has a set of default colors for the brush and fill colors. These default colors can be accessed easily and changed to suit your needs.

To work with the default colors:

1. Click the default colors icon **⑮** in either the Toolbox or the Color Mixer to set the brush and fill colors to their default settings.

2. Click the swap colors icon **⑯** in either the Toolbox or the Color Mixer to reverse the brush and fill colors.

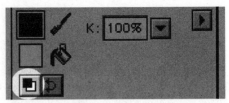

⑮ *Click the* **default colors icon** *(circled) in the Color Mixer to reset the brush and fill colors to their default setting.*

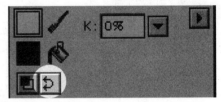

⑯ *Click the* **swap colors icon** *in the Color Mixer to reverse the brush and fill colors.*

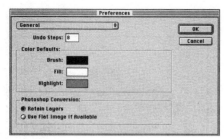

The **Preferences** *dialog box*

18 The **Eyedropper** *in the Toolbox*

19 *The Eyedropper sampling for a* **Fill color**

20 *The Eyedropper sampling for a* **Brush color**

21 *The* **Paint Bucket** *in the Toolbox*

To change the default colors:

1. Choose **File** > **Preferences** to open the Preferences dialog box **17**.

2. Click the color box for the Brush or Fill Color Defaults.

3. Use the color picker to choose a new default color.

4. Click OK to apply the changes.

The Eyedropper tool lets you pick colors from objects or images (*see page 141*).

To sample colors with the Eyedropper:

1. Choose the Eyedropper tool in the Toolbox **18**.

2. Position Eyedropper tool over the color you want to sample.

3. Click. The color appears as either the Fill or Brush color.

TIP When the Fill color is chosen (*see page 82*), the Eyedropper shows a black dot next to it **19**.

TIP When the Brush color is chosen in the Toolbox (*see page 98*), the Eyedropper shows a curved line next to it **20**.

The Paint Bucket lets you drop fills onto objects whether or not they are selected.

To drop colors with the Paint Bucket

1. Choose the Paint Bucket in the Toolbox **21**.

2. Click an object. The object fills with the currently selected Fill color in the Toolbox.

TIP If an object is selected, the Paint Bucket ignores the color in the Toolbox and fills with whatever fill, such as patterns or gradients, is in the selected object. (*See Chapter 7, "Fills."*)

Default Colors; Eyedropper; Paint Bucket

As you are working, you may want to know the color of an object or image. Fireworks lets you see the color anywhere in your document in the Info bar.

To use the Info bar:

1. Make sure the Info bar is open. If not, choose **Windows > Toolbar > Info**.

2. Pass the pointer over any objects. The Info bar displays the values for the color the pointer is over **㉒**.

3. Click the Info bar menu icon to open the Info Options dialog box **㉓**.

4. Use the Color Model list to change the way the Info bar displays the color values.

TIP Changing the way the Info bar displays colors does not actually change the color itself. Colors in Fireworks are not set until they are exported as a finished file (*see Chapter 15, "Basic Exporting"*).

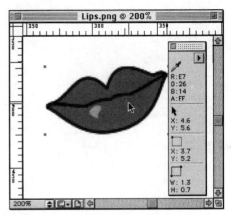

㉒ *The color readings of the* **Info bar**

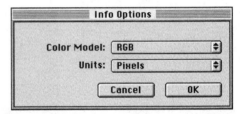

㉓ *The* **Info Options** *dialog box*

PATH TOOLS 4

Unlike bitmapped programs, Fireworks does not create images by coloring pixels. Fireworks creates images by creating paths. The eight path tools allow you to create different shapes that are then used as the basis of Fireworks images. If you are familiar with vector drawing programs such as Macromedia FreeHand, Adobe Illustrator, or CorelDraw, you will find it easy to understand the path tools in Fireworks. If you have never used a vector program, pay attention to this chapter because creating paths is the primary source of images in Fireworks.

In this chapter you will learn how to

Create a rectangle.

Create a rounded-corner rectangle.

Create an ellipse.

Create a polygon.

Create a star.

Create straight line segments.

Create curved line segments.

Retract the handle into a point.

Extend a handle out from a point.

Create an open path with the Pen.

Create a closed path with the Pen.

Create lines.

Create paths with the Brush tool.

Add to a brush path.

Modify a brush path.

Draw with the Pencil.

Soften the edges of Pencil lines.

Use the Auto Erase feature.

Add points to a path.

Delete points from a path.

Although it is called the Rectangle tool, this tool lets you create rectangles, squares, and rounded corner rectangles. With the Rectangle tool you can create buttons and banners for your Web graphics.

To create a rectangle:

1. Click the Rectangle tool in the Toolbox ❶. (If the Rectangle tool is not visible, press the pop-up group indicator to choose the Rectangle tool.)

2. Move the pointer to the document area. The cursor changes to the plus (+) sign indicating that you can draw the rectangle.

3. Drag diagonally from one corner to the other of the rectangle you want to draw.

TIP Hold the Shift key as you drag to constrain the rectangle into a square ❷.

TIP Hold the Option/Alt key as you drag to draw from the center point outward.

4. Release the mouse button to create the rectangle.

❶ *The* **Rectangle tool** *in the Toolbox*

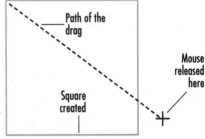

❷ **Holding the Shift key** *constrains the rectangle tool to creating a square even if the path of the drag is not along the correct diagonal of the square.*

Rectangle

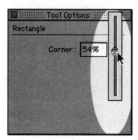

❸ *The* **Corner radius** *slider*

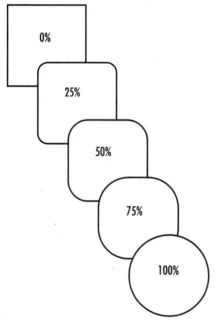

❹ *Rectangles drawn with different percentages for the corner radius*

❺ *The* **Ellipse tool** *in the Toolbox*

A rectangle with a rounded corner is a very popular look for buttons and other interactive Web elements.

To create a rounded-corner rectangle:

1. Double-click the Rectangle tool in the Toolbox. This opens the Tool Options for the Rectangle tool.

2. Drag the Corner slider to increase the size of the corner radius ❸.

TIP The size of the corner radius is a percentage of the length of the shorter side of the rectangle.

3. Drag as you would to create a regular rectangle. The corners of the rectangle are rounded by the percentage set for the corner radius ❹.

TIP The percentage size of the corner radius is set once you create the rounded-corner rectangle. If you scale the rectangle up or down (*see page* 67) the corner radius changes accordingly.

You can create ellipses or ovals using the Ellipse tool.

To create an ellipse:

1. Click the Ellipse tool in the Toolbox ❺. (If the Ellipse tool is not visible, press the pop-up group indicator to choose the Ellipse tool.)

2. Move the pointer to the document area.

3. Drag a line that defines the diameter of the ellipse.

TIP Hold the Shift key as you drag to constrain the ellipse into a circle.

TIP Hold the Option/Alt key as you drag to draw from the center point outward.

4. Release the mouse button to complete the ellipse.

Rounded-Corner Rectangle; Ellipse

Polygons give your Web graphics a special look. You use the Polygon tool to create both polygons and stars.

To create a polygon:

1. Click the Polygon tool in the Toolbox ❻. (If the Polygon tool is not visible, press the pop-up group indicator to choose the Polygon tool.)

2. Double-click the Polygon tool to display the Tool Options panel ❼.

3. Choose Polygon from the pop-up list.

4. Use the slider or enter a number from 3 to 25 in the field to set the number of sides for the polygon.

5. Move the pointer to the document area and drag. The point where you start the drag is the center of the polygon.

    TIP Hold the Shift key as you drag to constrain the orientation of the polygon to 45° increment angles.

6. Release the mouse button to create the polygon.

❻ *The* **Polygon tool** *in the Toolbox*

❼ *The* **Polygon tool** *options*

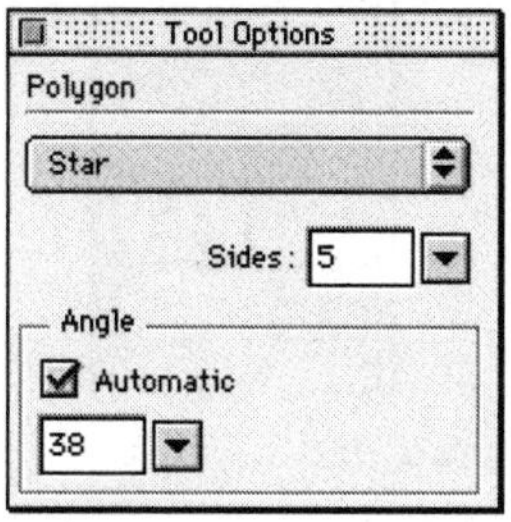

❽ *The Polygon tool set for the* **Star** *options*

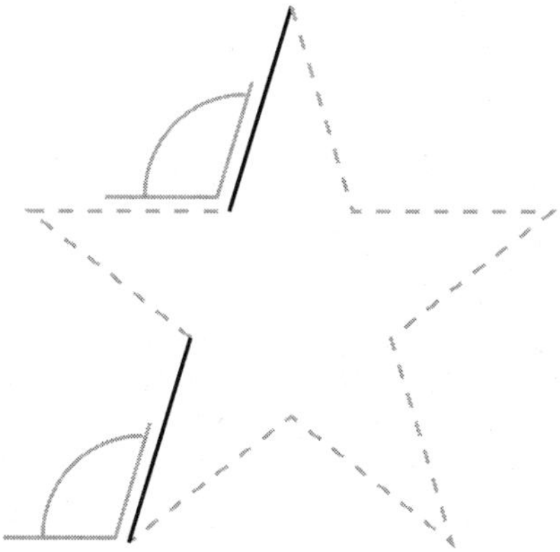

❾ *The two black segments are parallel as a result of setting the star to* **Automatic.**

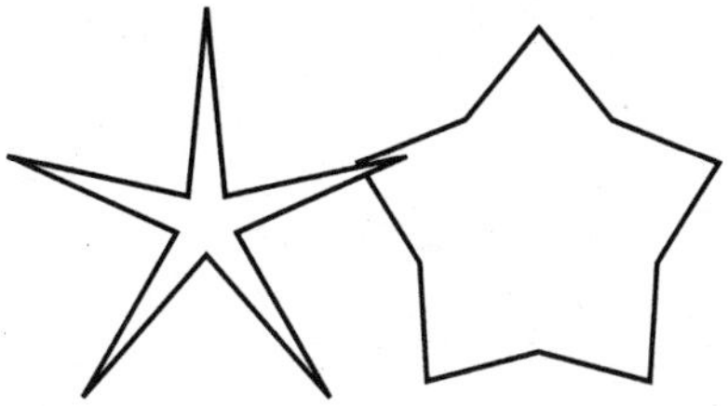

❿ *The difference between* **Acute** *and* **Obtuse angles** *for creating stars*

Fireworks also lets you create stars. When stars have many points they are sometimes called bursts. You can use bursts to call attention to special information.

To create a star:

1. Click the Polygon tool in the Toolbox. (If the Polygon tool is not visible, press the pop-up group indicator to choose the Polygon tool.)
2. Double-click the Polygon tool to display the Tool Options panel.
3. Choose Star from the pop-up list in the Tool Options. This adds the Angle controls to the panel ❽.
4. Use the slider or enter a number from 3 to 25 in the field to set the number of sides for the star.
5. Check Automatic to create stars with parallel line segments ❾.

   or

   Use the slider to set the angle of the points. Low settings create acute angles. High settings create obtuse angles ❿.

One of the most important tools in any vector program is its Pen tool. The Pen tool allows you to precisely create a wide variety of shapes. The Fireworks Pen tool is very similar to those found in Macromedia FreeHand, Adobe Illustrator, and Adobe Photoshop.

The best way to learn to use the pen is to start by creating straight segments.

To create a straight segment:

1. Click the Pen tool in the Toolbox **⓫**.

2. Move the pointer to the document area. The cursor changes to the plus (+) sign with a white square dot next to it. This indicates the start of the path **⓬**.

3. Click to create an anchor point for the first segment of the path.

4. Move the cursor to where you want the next anchor point of the path. The cursor changes to a plus sign without a dot next to it. This indicates that the next point is connected to the previous one.

5. Click. This connects the two anchor points with a straight line segment **⓭**.

6. Continue to create straight segments by repeating steps 4 and 5. (*See page 49 for how to finish the path.*)

⓫ *The* **Pen tool** *in the Toolbox*

⓬ *The* **start icon** *for the Pen tool*

⓭ *Clicking with the Pen tool creates* **straight segments.**

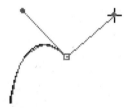

⓮ *Dragging with the Pen tool creates* **curved segments.**

⓯ *A path with a series of curved segments*

⓰ *Hold the Option/Alt key to pivot the handles which creates a* **corner curve.**

The next type of segment you can create is a curved segment. Think of a curved segment as the shape that a rollercoaster follows along a track.

To create a curved segment:

1. Click the Pen tool in the Toolbox.

2. Move the pointer to the document area. The cursor changes to the plus sign with a white square dot next to it.

3. Press and drag to create an anchor point with control handles.

4. Release the mouse button. The length and direction of the handle controls the height and direction of the curve **⓮**.

5. Move the cursor to where you want the next anchor point of the path. Drag to create the curved segment between the two anchor points.

6. Continue to create curved segments by repeating steps 3 and 4 **⓯**. (*See page 49 for how to finish the path.*)

Curves do not have to be smooth. A corner curve has an abrupt change in direction. The path of a bouncing ball is a corner curve.

To create a corner curve:

1. Press and drag to create an anchor point with control handles. Do not release the mouse button.

2. Hold the Option/Alt key and then move the mouse to pivot the second handle **⓰**.

3. Release the mouse button when the second handle is the correct length and direction.

4. Continue to create segments along the path.

Once you have created a curved segment with two handles, you can retract the second handle back into the anchor point. This makes the next segment of the path a straight segment.

To retract the handle into a point:

1. Drag to create an anchor point with two control handles.

2. Move the cursor back over the anchor point. A small arrow appears next to the plus sign.

3. Click. The handle retracts back into the anchor point **⑰**.

4. Continue the path with either straight segments or curved segments.

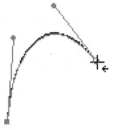

⑰ *Move the cursor back over a point and click to* **retract a handle** *along a curve.*

Once you click to create an anchor point with no control handles, you can extend a single handle out from that anchor point. This makes the next segment of the path a curved segment.

To extend a handle out from a point:

1. Click to create an anchor point with no control handles.

2. Move the pointer back over the anchor point you just created. A small arrow appears next to the plus sign.

3. Hold the Comand+Option keys (Mac) or Ctrl+Alt keys (Win) as you drag out from the anchor point **⑱**. A single control handle extends out from the anchor point.

4. Continue the path with either straight segments or curved segments.

⑱ *Hold the Command+Option keys (Mac) or Ctrl+Alt keys (Win) to* **extend a handle** *out from an anchor point.*

⓳ *An* **Open path**

⓴ *The* **Closed path** *icon*

㉑ *The* **Line tool** *in the Toolbox*

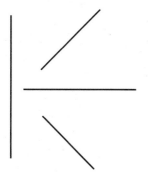

㉒ *The results of* **holding the Shift key** *while drawing with the Line tool*

There are two ways to finish a path in Fireworks. The first way is to leave the end points of the path open. A piece of string is a good example of an open path.

To create an open path:

1. Move the pen away from the last point of the path.

2. Hold the Command/Crl key and double-click. This leaves the path open **⓳** and allows you to continue using the Pen tool.

   or

   Switch to another tool in th toolbox. This leaves the path open.

The second way to finish a path is to join the last point of the path to the first. This creates a closed path. A rubber band is a good example of a closed path.

To create a closed path:

Move the cursor to the first anchor point of the path. The cursor changes to plus sign with a black square dot next to it **⓴**. Click to close the path.

You can use the Line tool to quickly create straight line segments.

To create a line:

1. Click the Line tool in the Toolbox **㉑**.

2. Move the pointer to the document area. The cursor changes to the plus sign.

3. Drag to set the length and direction of the line.

TIP Hold the Shift key to constrain the angle of the line to 45° increments **㉒**.

4. Release the mouse button to complete the line.

Fireworks also has a Brush tool that lets you draw more freely, without worrying about how and where you are placing anchor points.

To draw with the Brush:

1. Click the Brush tool in the Toolbox ❷❸.

2. Move the pointer to the document area. The cursor changes to the brush icon.

3. Drag to create a path that follows the movements of the mouse.

4. Release the mouse button to end the path.

TIP Release the mouse button where you started to close the path.

❷❸ *The Brush tool in the Toolbox*

Once you have created a path with Brush tool, you can add another brushstroke to the length of the path.

To add to a brush path:

1. Select the brush path. If you have just finished drawing the path, it will still be selected. You can also use the Pointer tool to select paths that were created previously (*see Chapter 5, "Selecting Paths"*).

2. Hold the Option/Alt key and move the Brush tool over one of the ends of the path. A plus sign appears next to the brush ❷❹.

3. Drag to extend the path. (Once you have started the drag, you can release the Option/Alt key.)

TIP You can use these same steps to add a segment created by the Pen, Line, or Pencil tools. (*See the next set of exercises for working with the Pencil tool.*)

❷❹ **Adding a brush stroke** *to an existing path*

㉕ *The* **Redraw Path tool** *in the Toolbox*

㉖ *The* **Redraw path icon**

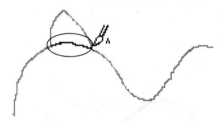

㉗ *The red line (circled) shows the original path as the Redraw Path tool creates the new path.*

Once you have created a path with Brush tool, you can modify the shape of the path.

To modify a brush path:

1. Select the brush path.

2. Press the pop-up group in the Toolbox to choose the Redraw Path tool **㉕**.

3. Move the tool to the point of the path that you want to redraw. A small triangle sign appears next to the brush icon **㉖**. This indicates that the path will be redrawn.

4. Drag to create the new shape of the path. A red line appears that indicates the part of the path that is modified **㉗**.

5. Release the mouse to redraw the path.

TIP Hold the Option/Alt key while using the Brush tool to temporarily switch to the Redraw Path tool.

TIP You can use these same steps to modify a segment created by the Pen, Line, or Pencil tools. (*See the next set of exercises for working with the Pencil tool.*)

TIP You can also modify the shape of a path by manipulating the the anchor points and control handles of the path. (*See Chapter 5, "Selecting Paths."*)

Modify a Brush Path

The Pencil tool lets you draw without worrying about placing anchor points or creating handles. The Pencil tool can also be used in the image editing mode to color individual pixels. (*For more information on working in the image editing mode see Chapter 11, "Pixel Images" and Chapter 12, "Pixel Tools."*)

㉘ *The* **Pencil Tool** *in the Toolbox*

To draw with the Pencil:

1. Click the Pencil tool in the Toolbox **㉘**.

2. Move the pointer to the document area. The cursor changes to a plus sign.

3. Drag to create a line that follows the movements of the mouse.

4. Release the mouse button to finish drawing the line.

TIP Release the mouse button where you started to close the path.

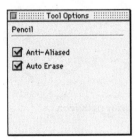

㉙ *The* **Pencil Tool** *options*

You can soften the look of Pencil lines by turning on the anti-aliasing option.

To anti-alias pencil lines:

1. Double-click the Pencil tool in the Toolbox to display the Tool Options for the Pencil **㉙**.

2. Click the Anti-Aliased option to soften the lines created by the pencil **㉚**.

TIP Anti-aliasing creates additional colors in the line create by the Pencil. This can add to the size of the final Web graphic.

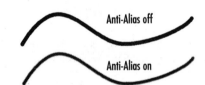

㉚ *The difference between drawing with the* **Anti-Aliasing option** *on and off*

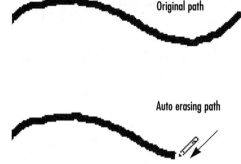

Original path

Auto erasing path

❸ *Dragging with the Pencil tool along a path with the **Auto Erase option** lets you erase the path by coloring it with the Fill color.*

The Auto Erase option lets you erase Pencil lines by drawing over them with the Fill color. (*For more information on Fill and Brush colors, see Chapter 7, "Fills" and Chapter 8, "Brushes."*)

To use the Auto Erase:

1. Click Auto Erase in the Pencil Tool Options.

2. Place the Pencil over a path colored with the current Brush color.

3. Drag the Pencil. The path changes from the Brush to the Fill color **❸**.

TIP When working in the path mode, the Auto-Erase option of the Pencil does not actually change the colors of the previously drawn path; rather it creates a new path on top of the first one.

TIP The Auto Erase option works best when the path does not have anti-aliasing turned on. This makes it easier to position the Pencil over a pixel colored exactly with the Brush color and not a shade created by anti-aliasing.

Auto Erase

As you work with paths, you may find that you need to add points to a path. This makes it much easier to reshape an existing path. Adding and deleting points on a path requires selecting the path with the Subselection tool. (*See Chapter 5, "Selecting Paths" for more information on working with the Subselection tool.*)

To add points to a path:

1. Use the Subselection tool to select the path with its points visible.

2. Bring the Pen on top of the segments where you want to add the point. A small caret (^) appears next to the cursor **32**.

3. Click. A new point appears.

Just as you can add points, you can delete points from a path.

To delete points from a path:

1. Select the path.

2. Use the Subselection tool to select the point or points.

3. Press the Delete/Backspace key on the keyboard. The point disappears from the path **33**.

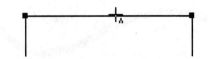

32 *Click with the Pen tool to* **add a point** *onto a path.*

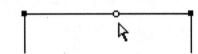

33 *A* selected **point on a path can be deleted** *by pressing the delete/backspace key.*

SELECTING PATHS 5

Once you have created objects using the path tools, you have many more options available. You can select and manipulate the individual points of the paths, Again, if you are familiar with a vector drawing program, you will find many of these exercises familiar. However, there are a few new tricks that Fireworks provides for selecting objects.

In this chapter you will learn how to

Use the Pointer tool.

Marquee selected objects.

Add or subtract objects from a selection.

Use the Subselection tool.

Use the Select Behind tool.

Use the Select menu commands.

Set the Mouse Highlight.

Group selected objects.

Select objects within groups.

Use the Subselect and Superselect commands.

Hide the highlight of selected objects.

Change the highlight color.

Several different tools help you select objects. The main selection aid is the Pointer tool. The Pointer tool selects objects as complete paths.

To use the Pointer tool:

1. Click the Pointer tool in the Toolbox **❶**.

   TIP Hold the Command/Ctrl key to temporarily access the Pointer tool. Release the key to return to the original tool.

2. Position the Pointer arrow over an object and click. A highlight color appears along the path indicating that the object is selected **❷**.

   TIP If the object has no fill color, you must click the path or brush color to select the object.

   TIP If you are working in the Draft Display mode (*see page 27*), you must click the path directly to select the object.

3. Hold the Shift key and click to select any additional objects.

4. Hold the Shift key and click to deselect any objects.

You can also select many objects at once by dragging a marquee with the Pointer tool.

To marquee selected objects:

1. Place the Pointer tool outside the area of the objects you want to select.

2. Drag diagnonally with the Pointer tool to create a rectangle that encloses your selection.

3. Release the mouse button to select any objects inside the rectangle **❸**.

❶ *The* **Pointer tool** *in the Toolbox*

Unselected   Selected

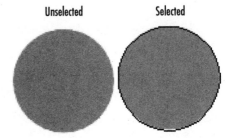

❷ *A highlight color appears on the path of a* **selected object.**

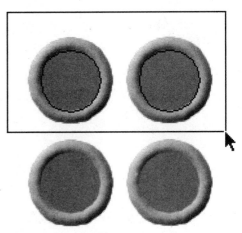

❸ *Drag with the Pointer tool to select objects within the* **rectangular marquee.**

❹ *The* **Subselection tool** *in the Toolbox*

Once you have objects selected, you can add objects to or subtract from them.

To add or subtract objects from a selection:

Hold the shift key and click with the Pointer tool. If the object is currently unselected, it will be added to the selected objects. If the object is current selected, it will be deselected from the selected objects.

TIP It may be easier to marquee select a group of objects and then use the Shift key to deselect the one or two you do not want as part of the selection.

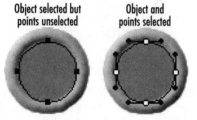

Object selected but points unselected   Object and points selected

❺ *The* **Subselection tool** *allows you to see the individual anchor points of a selected object. Clicking specific points selects them.*

Fireworks creates paths with anchor points defining the shape of the path. You can use the Subselection tool to select those individual points and manipulate them to change the shape of the objects.

To use the Subselection tool:

1. Click the Subselection tool in the Toolbox ❹.

2. Select any object either by clicking or dragging a marquee. The anchor points of the object are selected.

TIP Anchor points filled with the highlight color are unselected. Anchor points that are white are selected points ❺.

3. Use the Subselection tool to drag any selected points, without moving the unselected points ❻.

TIP If you switch from the Pointer tool to the Subselection tool while an object is already selected, you see the anchor points for that object.

❻ **Drag with the Subselection tool** *to change the position of anchor points.*

Because transparency is so important in creating Fireworks graphics, you may find that your artwork consists of many objects stacked on top of each other. This could make it difficult to select an object behind the rest. The Select Behind tool makes it easy to select through other objects to one at the back.

❼ *The* **Select Behind tool** *in the Toolbox*

To use the Select Behind tool:

1. Press the pop-up group for the Pointer tool to choose the Select Behind tool ❼.

2. Click with the Select Behind tool over the objects you want to select. The first click selects the object on top of the others.

3. Click as many times as necessary to select the object behind the others ❽.

TIP Hold the Shift key as you click to add each object to the selection.

❽ *The Select Behind tool was used to select the star behind the other two objects. The first click selected the square. The second click selected the circle. The third click selected the star.*

In addition to the selection tools, the commands in the Select menu allow you to select and deselect objects.

To use the Select menu commands:

Choose **Select > All** to select all the objects in a file. Choose **Select > None** to deselect any selected objects. These commands can also be used when working in the Image Editing mode (*see Chapter 11, "Pixel Images"*).

TIP You can also deselect any objects in a file by clicking the empty space in a document with the Pointer tool.

⑨ *The* **Mouse Highlight option** *for the selection tools*

If you are working with many objects, all overlapping one other, it may be difficult to know which object you are about to select. The Mouse Highlight feature allows you to know which object is about to be selected with the next click.

To set the Mouse Highlight:

1. Double-click the Pointer, Subselection, or Select Behind tool to open the Tool Options panel.

2. Select Mouse Highlight in the panel ⑨.

3. Move the selection tool over an object. A red line appears around the object that can be selected with the next mouse click.

⑩ *A* **Grouped object** *displays four points when selected.*

Once you have created several objects, you may find it easier to select all those objects together as a single unit, or group.

To group selected objects:

1. Select two or more objects.

2. Choose **Select**>**Group**. Small anchor points appear around the object indicating they are a group ⑩.

TIP Fireworks lets you group a single object. This allows you to apply more than one effect to a single object (*see Chapter 9, "Effects"*).

3. You can add objects to the group by selecting the group and the objects and choosing the group command.

TIP Choose **Select**>**Ungroup** to release the objects from the group.

TIP (Win) You can also use the Group/ Ungroup icons on the Modify toolbar.

When you have objects in a group, you may want to select an specific object within the group.

To select objects within groups:

Hold the Option/Alt key and use the Pointer, Subselection, or Select Behind tool to select an individual object from a group.

TIP Hold the Shift and Option/Alt keys to add other items to the selection.

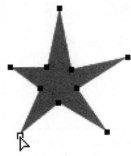

⓫ *The* **Hide Edges** *command hides the highlight along a path but keeps the anchor points and control handles visible when you're using the Subselection tool.*

Fireworks also has two menu commands, Subselect and Superselect, that make it easy to work with groups.

To use the Subselect command:

Select a group and then choose **Select > Subselect**. This breaks the grouped selection into its individual elements.

To use the Superselect command:

Select a single item in a group and then choose **Select > Superselect**. This selects the group that contained the selection.

TIP You can reapply both the Subselect and Superselect commands to further select groups within groups.

If you find the highlight color interferes with your work, you can hide the highlight color while keeping the object selected.

To hide the highlight of selected objects:

Choose **View > Hide Edges**. This hides the highlight along the path of an object. To reveal the highlight, choose **View > Hide Edges** when there is a checkmark in front of the command.

TIP Anchor points and control handles are still visible when the Hide Edges command is applied **⓫**.

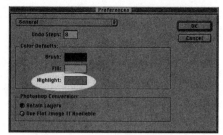

⓬ *Click the* **Highlight** *box (circled) in the Preferences dialog box to change the color of the path highlight.*

You may not be able to see the path highlight color if it is too similar to the color of the brush stroke around an object. You can use the Preferences to change the path highlight color.

To change the highlight color:

1. Choose **File > Preferences** to open the Preferences dialog box **⓬**.

2. Click the Highlight color box. The Color picker dialog box appears.

3. Choose the color for the highlight and then click OK.

TIP The highlight color is an application preference. Changing it changes the highlight color for all Fireworks documents.

Change Highlight

WORKING WITH OBJECTS 6

Once you have created objects, there are many different ways you can work with those objects. Some of the ways you can work with objects change the shape of the objects themselves. Other ways you can work with objects is to change their relationship to other objects. Finally, you can change the properties of objects so that they change their appearance.

In this chapter you will learn how to

Move an object by eye.

Move an object numerically.

Copy and paste an object.

Clone an object.

Duplicate an object.

Drag and drop between documents.

Copy an object as you move it.

Scale an object.

Skew an object.

Distort an object.

Rotate an object.

Use the Transform commands.

Use the Freeform tool.

Use the Reshape Area tool.

Use the Eraser tool.

Align objects.

Use the Arrange commands.

Work with the Layer panel.

Use Single Layer Editing.

Move objects between layers.

If you can select it, you can move it simply by dragging the mouse.

To move an object by eye:

1. Select the object.
2. Using any of the selection tools, drag the object to the new position.

TIP Drag anywhere on the object except on a point.

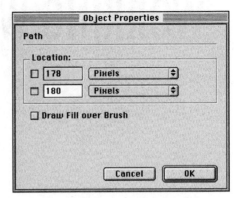

❶ *The* **Object Properties** *dialog box lets you change the position of an object.*

You can also move any object by changing its Object Properties coordinates.

To move an object numerically:

1. Select the object.
2. Choose **Modify > Object Properties**. The Object Properties dialog box appears ❶.
3. Change the number in the first field to move the left edge of the object to a specific position.
4. Change the number in the second field to move the top edge of the object to a specific position.
5. Click OK. The object moves into the position.

You can copy and paste objects in Fireworks as you would in other graphics programs. There are a few special features you should know.

To copy and paste an object:

1. Select the object.
2. Choose **Edit > Copy**.
3. Choose **Edit > Paste** to paste the object into the same position as the original.

TIP Although it may not seem very useful, pasting an object into the same position is helpful when creating rollover buttons (*see Chapter 18, "Rollovers"*).

Move an Object; Copy and Paste

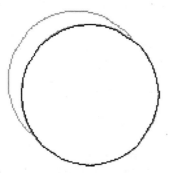

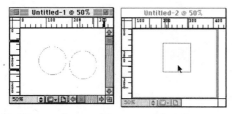

In addition to copy and paste, you can make copies of objects using the Duplicate and Clone commands.

To clone an object:

1. Select the object.

2. Choose **Edit > Clone**. A duplicate of the object appears in exactly the same position as the original.

❷ *The* **Duplicate** *command copies the selected object.*

To duplicate an object:

1. Select the object.

2. Choose **Edit > Duplicate**. A duplicate of the object appears slightly offset from the original ❷.

❸ *You can* **drag and drop** *an object from one document to another.*

Another way to duplicate objects from one document to another is to use the drag-and-drop feature.

To drag and drop an object:

1. Position two document windows so that both are visible.

2. Use any of the selection tools to move an object from one document to the other.

3. Release the mouse button. A copy of the object appears in the second document ❸.

Clone; Duplicate; Drag and Drop

Another technique allows you to copy an object as you move it. On the Macintosh this technique can be called an Option-Drag. On Windows, it can be called an Alt-Drag. This is one of the quickest ways to duplicate vector objects.

To copy an object as you move it:

1. Choose any of the selection tools.

2. Hold the Option/Alt key as you move the object. A small plus sign (+) appears next to the arrow as you move the object ❹.

3. Release the mouse button. A copy of the object appears.

TIP The Clone, Duplicate, Drag and Drop, and Option/Alt-Drag actions all leave the contents of the Clipboard unchanged. This can help avoid using extra RAM to hold the contents of a large clipboard.

❹ **Holding the Option/Alt keys** *as you move an object creates a copy of that object.*

⑤ *The* **Scale tool** *in the Toolbox*

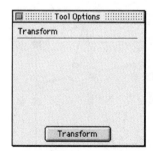

⑥ **Drag a corner handle with the Scale tool** *to change the horizontal and vertical dimensions of the object porportionally.*

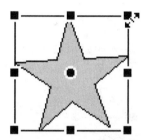

⑦ *The* **Transform button** *in the Tool Options panel*

Transformations are actions that change the size, shape, or orientation of an object. Fireworks provides many different ways to transform objects. Scaling transforms an object by changing its size.

To scale an object:

1. Choose the Scale tool in the Toolbox **⑤**.

   or

   Choose **Modify > Transform > Scale**. The transformation handles appear around the object.

2. Place the cursor directly over any of the handles. A small double-headed arrow appears.

3. Drag toward the object to make it smaller or away from the object to make it bigger **⑥**.

   TIP Drag one of the corner handles to scale both the horizontal and vertical dimensions of the object.

   TIP Drag the edge handles to change just the horizontal or vertical dimensions of the object.

4. Double-click within the bounding box of the transformation handles to apply the transformation.

   or

   Click the Transform button in the Tool Options panel **⑦**.

   TIP To leave the transformation mode without applying the transformation, switch to any other tool in the Toolbox or press the Esc key on the keyboard.

Scale

The skewing transformation moves two sides of the bounding box together or two control handles in opposite directions. Skewing creates 3-dimensional effects for objects or for text (*see page 121*).

To skew an object:

1. Choose the Skew tool in the Toolbox ❽.

   or

   Choose **Modify > Transform > Skew**. The transformation handles appear around the object.

2. Place the cursor directly over any of the handles.

3. Drag one of the corner handles in or out to move that handle and the one opposite it. This changes the dimension of that side of the object ❾.

4. Drag one of the side handles to change the angle of that side of the object ❿.

5. Double-click within the box created by the transformation handles to apply the transformation.

   or

   Click the Transform button in the Tool Options panel.

TIP To leave the transformation mode without applying the transformation, switch to any other tool in the Toolbox or press the Esc key on the keyboard.

❽ *The* **Skew tool** *in the Toolbox*

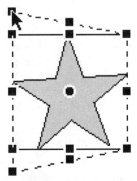

❾ **Drag a corner handle with the Skew tool** *to change the dimension of that side of the object.*

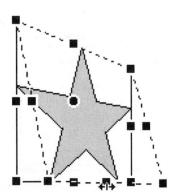

❿ **Drag a side handle with the Skew tool** *to change the angles along that side of the object.*

Skew

⑪ The **Distort tool** *in the Toolbox*

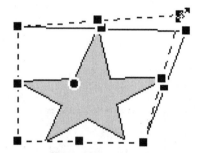

⑫ **Drag a handle with the Distort tool** *to change the shape of an object.*

The distortion transformation allows you to distort the shape of object by changing the shape of the box that defines the object.

To distort an object:

1. Choose the Distort tool in the Toolbox **⑪**.

   or

   Choose **Modify > Transform > Distort**. The transformation handles appear around the object.

2. Place the cursor directly over any of the handles.

3. Drag one of the side handles to change the shape of the object **⑫**.

4. Double-click within the box created by the transformation handles to apply the transformation.

   or

   Click the Transform button in the Tool Options panel.

TIP To leave the transformation mode without applying the transformation, switch to any other tool in the Toolbox or press the Esc key on the keyboard.

Distort

An additional transformation, rotation, is available when you use any of the three transformation tools.

To rotate an object:

1. Choose any of the Transformation tools.

2. Position the cursor outside of the handles. A rounded arrow appears.

3. Drag either clockwise or counter-clockwise to rotate the object **⑬**.

TIP Move the small transformation circle to change the point around which the object rotates.

4. Double-click within the box created by the transformation handles to apply the transformation.

    or

    Click the Transform button in the Tool Options panel.

TIP To leave the transformation mode without applying the transformation, switch to any other tool in the Toolbox or press the Esc key on the keyboard.

You can also move an object while in the transformation mode.

To move an object in the transformation mode:

1. Choose any of the Transformation tools.

2. Position the cursor inside the box created by the transformation handles. A four-headed arrow appears **⑭**.

3. Drag to move the object.

4. Continue working with the transformation tools or apply the transformation by double-clicking within the box created by the transformation handles.

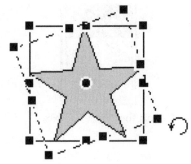

⑬ Drag with the Rotation icon *to change the orientation of an object.*

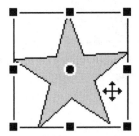

⑭ *The* **four-headed arrow** *appears while moving an object in the transformation mode.*

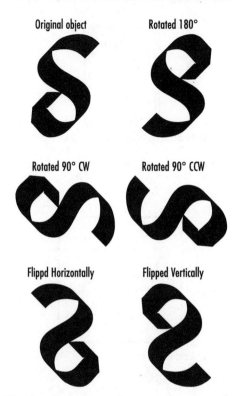

Original object   Rotated 180°

Rotated 90° CW   Rotated 90° CCW

Flippd Horizontally   Flipped Vertically

⑮ *The* **effect of Transform menu commands** *on the original object (upper left).*

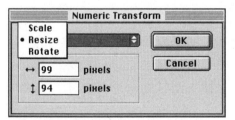

⑯ *The* **Numeric Transform** *dialog box*

Fireworks also gives you a set of transformation menu commands that make it easy to rotate or flip objects **⑮**.

To use the Transform menu commands:

1. Select an object.

2. Rotate or flip the object by choosing a command from the **Modify > Transform** menu, for example, **Modify > Transform > Rotate 180°**.

TIP (Win) You can also use the rotate icons on the Modify toolbar to easily apply rotations.

The Numeric Transform dialog box makes it easy to scale, resize, or rotate an object using numeric values, rather than by judging by eye.

To use the Numeric Transform dialog box:

1. Select an object.

2. Rotate or flip the object by choosing a command from the **Modify > Transform > Numeric Transform**. The Numeric Transform dialog box appears **⑯**

3. Use the pop-up list to choose Scale, Resize, or Rotate.

4. In the Scale mode, enter the percentage of change in the width or height fields.

   or

   In the Resize mode, enter the pixel amount in the width or height fields.

   or

   In the Rotate mode, use the wheel or enter the angle amount in the field.

5. Click OK to apply the transformation.

TIP Both Scale and Resize change the size of the object. Scale does so using percentages. Resize does so by changing the pixel dimensions.

Once you have created an object, you may find it difficult to work with the control handles to reshape the path. The Freeform tool allows you to change the shape of an object without worrying about adding or modifying points.

To set the Freeform tool options:

1. Choose the Freeform tool in the Toolbox .

2. Double-click the Freeform tool in the Toolbox to open the Tool Options panel ⓲.

3. Use the slider or click in the Size field to set the size of tool. This controls how large an area is pushed by the tool.

4. If you have a pressure-sensitive pen and tablet, click Pressure to allow your pressure on the tablet to affect the size of the effect.

TIP If you do not have a pressure-sensitive tablet, press the 1, [, or left-arrow key as you drag to decrease the size of the Freeform tool effect.

TIP If you do not have a pressure-sensitive tablet, press the 2,], or right-arrow key as you drag to increase the size of the Freeform tool effect.

⓱ *The **Freeform tool** in the Toolbox*

⓲ *The **Freeform tool** options*

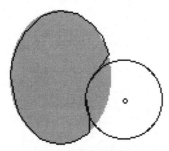

⑲ *The* **Push Freeform tool** *icon*

⑳ *The* **Push Freeform tool** *allows you to push on the edges of an object to reshape it.*

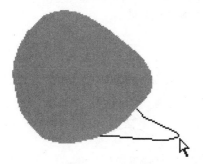

㉑ *The* **Pull Freeform tool** *icon*

㉒ *The* **Pull Freeform tool** *allows you to pull out segments from an object.*

There are two modes to the Freeform tool: the Push mode and the Pull mode. In the Push mode the Freeform tool acts like a rolling pin to modify the shape of the path.

To use the Freeform tool in the Push mode:

1. Set the Freeform tool options, as described on page 72.

2. Move the cursor near, but not on, the edge of a selected object. The cursor displays the Push icon, an arrow with a circle next to it **⑲**.

3. Drag around the edge of the object. The shape of the object changes accordingly **⑳**.

TIP The Push Freeform tool can work from either the inside or the outside of an object.

TIP Check Preview to turn off the highlight color on the object as you use the Freeform tool.

In the Pull mode the Freeform tool acts like a magnet that pulls out new segments from the path.

To use the Freeform tool in the Pull mode:

1. Set the Freeform tool options, as described on page 72.

2. Move the cursor to the edge of a selected object. The cursor displays the Pull icon **㉑**.

3. Drag in or out from the edge of the object. The shape of the object changes accordingly **㉒**.

The Reshape Area tool also lets you distort paths without manually adding or modifying anchor points or handles.

To set the Reshape Area tool options:

1. Choose the Reshape Area tool in the Toolbox ㉓.

2. Double-click the Reshape Area tool in the Toolbox to open the Tool Options panel ㉔.

3. Use the slider or click in the Size field to set the size of the Reshape Area tool. The greater the amount, the larger the area that the tool distorts ㉕.

4. Use the slider or click in the Strength field to set how long the tool will work during a drag—the greater the amount, the longer the tool distorts the path ㉖.

5. Use the slider or click in the Precision field to set the precision amount—the greater the amount, the more sensitive the tool is to movements of the mouse.

6. If you have a pressure-sensitive tablet, check the Size or Strength boxes to set how the pressure on the tablet affects the tool.

TIP If you do not have a pressure-sensitive tablet, press the 1, [, or left-arrow key as you drag to decrease the size of the Freeform tool effect.

TIP If you do not have a pressure-sensitive tablet, press the 2,], or right-arrow key as you drag to increase the size of the Freeform tool effect.

㉓ *The* **Reshape Area tool** *in the Toolbox*

㉔ *The options for the* **Reshape Area tool**

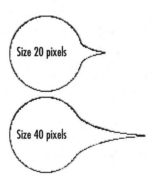

㉕ *The effect of changing the* size **of the Reshape Area tool**

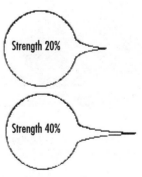

㉖ *The effect of changing the* **strength of the Reshape Area tool**

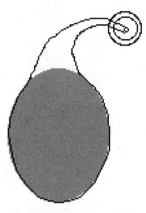

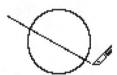

㉗ *The **Reshape Area tool** allows you to distort the path of objects.*

㉘ *The **Eraser tool** in the Toolbox*

㉙ *Cutting an object with the Eraser tool*

The Reshape Area tool modifies paths as if they were taffy. The size of the tool controls the amount that is pulled. The strength of the tool controls the length of the pull.

To use the Reshape Area tool:

1. Choose the Reshape Area tool.

2. Position the tool either inside or outside the path.

3. Drag to reshape the path **㉗**.

You can also modify paths by cutting them with the Eraser tool.

To use the Eraser tool:

1. Choose the Eraser tool in the Toolbox **㉘**.

2. Drag the Eraser tool across a path. This cuts the path **㉙**.

TIP Segments created by the Eraser tool can be moved away from the other objects with any of the selection tools.

TIP The Eraser tool also erases pixels in the Image Editing mode (*see page 140*).

TIP The Eraser tool has the look of an X-acto knife when cutting objects. It has the look of a rubber eraser when erasing pixels.

Reshape Area Tool; Eraser Tool

You can use the Align menu commands to align the objects or distribute them along the horizontal or vertical axis ㉚–㉝.

To use the Align menu commands:

1. Select two or more objects to align.

   or

   Select three or more objects to distribute.

2. Align or distribute the objects by choosing a command from the Modify > **Align** menu, for example, Modify > **Align** > **Left**.

TIP Fireworks uses the left-most object to align to the left and the right-most object to align to the right.

TIP Fireworks uses the topmost object to align to the top and the bottommost object to align to the bottom.

The Modify toolbar (Win) gives you icons to apply many of the object commands. All the Align commands are available in a pop-up list on the Modify toolbar.

To use the Align pop-up list (Win):

1. Select two or more objects to align.

   or

   Select three or more objects to distribute.

2. Press the Align icon on the Modify toolbar ㉞ and choose the alignment or distribute command.

㉚ The **Align Commands** *for the vertical axis*

㉛ The **Align Commands** *for the horizontal axis*

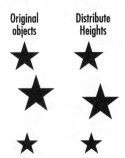

㉜ *The effect of applying the* **Distribute Heights** *command*

㉝ *The effect of applying the* **Distribute Widths** *command*

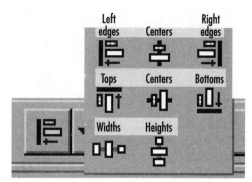

❸❹ *The* **Align pop-up list** *on the Modify toolbar (Win)*

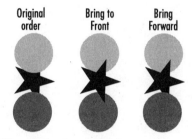

❸❺ *The results of applying the* **Arrange menu commands** *to the star*

Just as in other vector programs, the order in which objects appear depends on the order in which they were created. Objects that were created first are at the back of the file. Objects that were created later are in front. You can also change the order of the objects using the Arrange menu commands ❸❺. Objects can be moved to the front or back of their layer.

To send objects to the front or back of a layer:

1. Select the object.

2. Choose **Modify** > **Arrange** > **Bring to Front** to move the object in front of all the other objects on that layer.

   or

   Choose **Modify** > **Arrange** > **Send to Back** to move the object behind all the other objects on that layer.

TIP (Win) You can also use the Front/Back icons on the Modify toolbar to easily move objects within a layer.

Objects can also be moved forward or backward one place at a time in their layer.

To move objects forward or backward in a layer:

1. Select the object.

2. Choose **Modify** > **Arrange** > **Bring Forward** to move the object in front of the next object in the layer.

   or

   Choose **Modify** > **Arrange** > **Send Backward** to move the object behind the next object in the layer.

3. Repeat as necessary to put the object where you want it.

TIP (Win) You can also use the Forward/Backward icons on the Modify toolbar to easily move objects in front or behind each other.

As you add more objects to your documents, you may want to take advantage of the Fireworks Layers panel. This panel lets you show and hide objects on each of the layers, lock the layers from changes, and change the order in which objects appear.

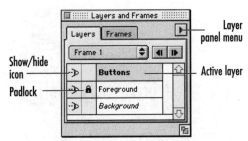

36 *The* Layers panel

To work with the Layers panel:

1. Open the Layers panel by choosing **Window>Layers 36**. The two default` layers, Foreground and Background, appear in the panel.

TIP The Background layer acts like the canvas of a painting program. Vector objects cannot be placed on this layer, only pixel images. (*For more information on working with the image editing aspects of Fireworks, see Chapter 11, "Pixel Images" and Chapter 12, "Pixel Tools."*)

2. To make all the objects on a layer invisible, click the Show/hide icon for that layer.

TIP To make all the layers invisible, hold the Option/Alt key as you click the view icon for any layer.

3. To prevent any objects on a layer from being selected, click the space in the lock area. A padlock icon appears indicating the layer is locked.

TIP Click the layer's padlock icon to unlock the layer.

4. Click the name of a layer to make that layer the current active layer. Any objects created are then automatically on that layer.

5. Drag the name of a layer up or down to a new position in the panel to move the that layer to a new position.

TIP The Background layer is always the rearmost layer in the document.

Layers Panel

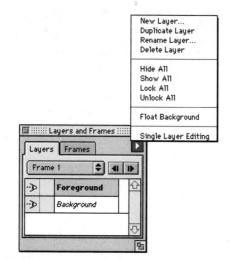

New Layer...
Duplicate Layer
Rename Layer...
Delete Layer

Hide All
Show All
Lock All
Unlock All

Float Background

Single Layer Editing

⑳ *The* Layers panel menu

The Layers panel menu controls additional features of the Layers panel.

To use the Layers panel menu:

1. Press the triangle at the top of the Layers panel to view the Layers panel menu ⑳.

2. Choose New Layer to open the Add Layer dialog box where you can name the new layer.

3. Choose Duplicate Layer to duplicate the layer currently selected along with its contents.

4. Choose Rename Layer to change the name of the currently selected layer.

TIP Double-click the name of a layer to change its name.

5. Choose Hide All or Show All to change the display status of all the layers in the document.

6. Lock All or Unlock All to change the protection applied to all the layers in the document.

Fireworks also has a special mode called Single Layer Editing. Single Layer Editing makes it easier to work only with the objects on one layer without having to lock the other layers.

To use Single Layer Editing:

Choose Single Layer Editing from the Layers panel menu. This makes the currently selected layer the only layer that can be worked on. Objects on other layers cannot be selected. To select objects on other layers, you need to select the layer in the Layers panel.

You can also move objects from one layer to another.

To move an object between layers:

1. Select the object. A small square appears next to the name of the layer that the object is on.

2. Drag the small square to the layer where you want the object ⓷.

[TIP] Objects can also be copied and pasted from one layer to another.

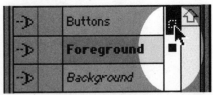

⓷ Drag the small object square *to move an object from one layer to another.*

FILLS 7

Vector objects in Fireworks act like
containers that you can fill with colors,
patterns, or gradients. Fireworks also
lets you manipulate objects so that the
objects display their fills in different ways.
This means that Fireworks gives you more
choices for filling objects than ordinary
vector programs.

In this chapter you will learn how to

Apply a solid color fill.

Apply the None fill setting.

Change the edges of a fill.

Apply a gradient fill.

Edit a gradient fill.

Save a gradient fill.

Delete a gradient fill.

Change the appearance of a gradient.

Apply a pattern fill.

Add patterns.

Apply a texture to a fill.

Add textures.

Use the Join command.

Use the Split command.

Change the object transparency.

Change the Blending modes.

Use Paste Inside to mask objects.

Use the Mask Group.

Move objects within a mask.

Paste attributes from one object to
another.

There are two different ways to style objects in Fireworks; fills and brushes. Fills are the colors, patterns and gradients that are applied inside paths.

To apply a solid color fill:

1. Choose **Window**>**Fill** to open the Fill panel.

   or

   Click the Fill panel tab to change from the Brush or Effects panel.

2. Choose Solid from the Fill category pop-up list. This displays the options for solid fills ❶.

3. Click the button state box to set the Color Mixer to the fill mode.

TIP You can also use the buttons in the Color Mixer or the Toolbox to set the Color Mixer to the fill mode.

4. Use the Color Mixer to select a color. (*For more information on working with the Color Mixer, see Chapter 3, "Colors."*)

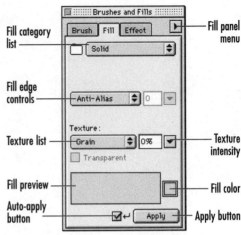

Fill category list — Fill panel menu

Fill edge controls

Texture list — Texture intensity

Fill preview — Fill color

Auto-apply button — Apply button

❶ *The* **Fill** *panel*

You can also set an object to have no fill. This makes the inside of the object completely transparent.

To apply the None fill setting:

Choose None from the Fill category pop-up list. This changes the fill of the object to completely transparent ❷.

TIP Click the edge to select an object with a None fill, or use a selection marquee.

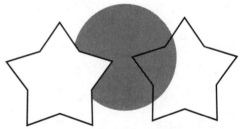

❷ *The difference between a white fill and a* **fill of None** *becomes obvious when the objects appear over another image.*

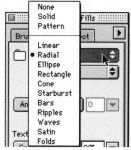

❸ *The three different* **Edge choices**

❹ *The* **Gradient category** *list*

Once you have filled an object, you can control how the edges of the object are filled.

To change the edges of a fill:

1. Select and fill an object.

2. Use the Fill-edge list to change the edge treatment of the fill ❸.

• Choose Hard-edge to leave the edge of the object as single-colored pixels.

• Choose Anti-alias to soften the edge of the object.

• Choose Feather and then use the slider to blur the edge of the object.

TIP The feather amount is in pixels and is applied equally to both sides of the edge of the path.

In addition to solid colors, Fireworks lets you fill objects with gradients, which gradually blend one color into another. You can apply the preset gradients that ship with Fireworks or create your own gradients.

To apply a gradient fill:

1. Select an object.

2. Choose one of the preset gradient fills from the Fill category pop-up list ❹.

TIP Each of the gradient presets controls how the colors of the gradients are manipulated. These presets control the shape and number of blends of the gradient. They do not control the colors or number of colors of the gradient. (*For a printout of the default settings of the preset gradients, see Appendix A.*)

3. To change the colors of the gradient, choose one of the gradient names ❺.

❺ *The* **Gradient names** *list*

The gradient names control the colors that are blended in the gradient. You can change those colors by editing the gradient. Once you edit the gradient, you can then save it under a new name.

To edit a gradient fill:

1. With a gradient selected, choose Edit gradient from the Fill panel menu ❻. This opens the Edit Gradient dialog box ❼.

2. Click one of the square gradient controls along the gradient ramp. Drag the control to change the position of the color.

3. Click in the empty area below the gradient ramp to add a new gradient control.

   TIP To delete a gradient control, drag it off of the area below the ramp.

4. Double-click the gradient control to open the Color Mixer. Choose the color you want and then click OK to apply the color to the gradient.

5. Use the preset pop-up list to change the colors in the gradient. (These are the same presets listed in the Fill panel menu.)

6. Click OK to apply the changes to the gradient.

   TIP For a color printout of the default gradient colors, see the color insert.

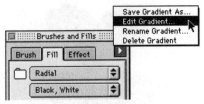

❻ *The* **Fill panel menu**

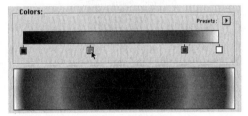

❼ *The* **Edit Gradient** *dialog box*

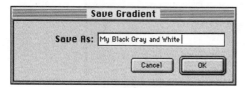

❽ *The* **Save Gradient** *dialog box*

Once you have changed the colors of a gradient, a plus sign appears next to its name. This indicates that the current gradient has not been saved as one of the gradient presets. If you want to use the gradient in other Fireworks documents, you need to save the gradient preset.

To save a gradient:

1. Choose Save Gradient As from the Fill panel menu. This opens the Save Gradient dialog box **❽**.

2. Give the gradient a name and then click OK.

TIP If you give the gradient a new name, you add a new preset to the list.

TIP If you give the gradient the same name as an existing gradient, a dialog box appears asking if you want to replace the original gradient with the new setting.

You can also delete gradients from the Fill panel menu.

To delete a gradient fill:

1. Select the gradient preset you want to delete.

2. Choose Delete Gradient from the Fill panel menu. A dialog box appears asking you to confirm the deletion of the gradient.

3. Click OK. The gradient is deleted from the list.

Save a Gradient; Delete a Gradient

In addition to controlling the colors in a gradient, you can also change the appearance of a gradient by changing its direction, length, and center.

To change the appearance of a gradient:

1. Select an object filled with a gradient.

2. Click the Paint Bucket tool in the Toolbox ❾. The Vector controls appear in the object ❿.

3. Move the circle control to change the start point of the gradient ⓫.

4. Drag the square control to change the end point of the gradient ⓬.

TIP Some gradients provide two control handles to control two axis of the gradient.

5. Drag the line of the control to change the rotation of the gradient ⓭.

TIP Double-click with the Paint Bucket tool to reset the Vector controls to the default setting.

❾ *The* **Paint Bucket** *in the Toolbox*

❿ *The* **Vector controls** *over a gradient*

⓫ *The* **Circle control** *defines the start point of a gradient.*

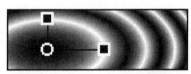

⓬ *The* **Square control** *defines the end point of the gradient. A short gradient repeats to fill the object.*

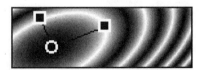

⓭ *The* **Angle of the controls** *defines the rotation of the gradient.*

Change a Gradient

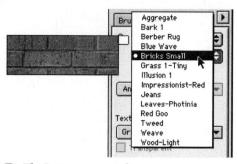

⑭ *The* **Patterns** *pop-up list*

In addition to gradients, Fireworks has a set of patterns that you can apply as the fill of objects.

To apply a pattern fill:

1. Choose pattern from the Fill category pop-up list. A second Fill name pop-up list appears.

2. Choose one of the preset pattern fills from the pattern list **⑭**. (*For a complete printout of all the default patterns, see Appendix A.*)

TIP A small preview appears next to each name as you move through the list.

TIP The Vector controls can also be used to modify the appearance of patterns as well as gradients (*see previous page*).

Patterns in Fireworks are simply images saved in the PNG format. If you have artwork from a scanner, or artwork created in another program, you can use that artwork as a pattern fill in Fireworks.

To add patterns:

1. Scan or create artwork that can be tiled as a pattern.

2. Give the file a name and save it as a PNG file.

3. Put the PNG file in the Patterns folder (Fireworks: Settings: Patterns). The name of the file appears as the name of the texture in the pop-up list.

Patterns; Add Patterns

Textures change the intensity of fills. You can apply textures to any of the fills—solids, patterns, or gradients. Once a texture is applied to a fill, you can then change the intensity of the texture.

To apply textures to a fill:

1. Choose one of the textures from the Texture pop-up list . (*For a complete printout of all the default textures, see Appendix A.*)

TIP There is always a texture applied to every fill. However, with an intensity of 0% the effect of the texture is not visible.

2. Use the slider or enter a number in the Intensity field to see the effects of the texture on the fill .

3. Check Transparent to allow background objects to appear in the light-colored areas of the texture 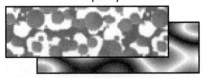.

⓯ *The* **Textures** *pop-up list*

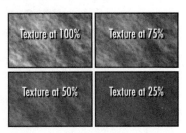

⓰ *Difference settings of the Parchment texture on a solid fill*

Transparency off

Transparency on

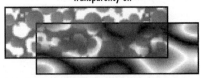

⓱ *The effect of the* **Transparent** *settings for a texture*

Textures

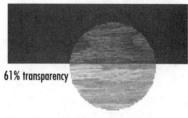

⑱ *The* Opacity *panel*

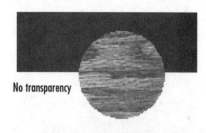

No transparency

61% transparency

⑲ *The effects of* adding transparency *to an object*

Like patterns, you can bring in textures from other applications to use within Fireworks.

To add textures:

1. Scan or create artwork that can be tiled as a texture.

2. Save the file as an Indexed Color or Grayscale document.

3. Give the file a name and save it as a PNG file.

4. Put the PNG file in the Textures folder (Fireworks: Settings: Textures). The name of the file appears as the name of the texture in the pop-up list.

Not only can you change the fill of objects, you can also control the transparency of each object in Fireworks.

To change the object transparency:

1. Choose **Window** > **Toolbars** > **Opacity** to open the Opacity panel **⑱**.

2. Select the object you want to change.

3. Use the slider or change the amount in the Transparency field. The change is applied automa tically **⑲**.

Add Textures; Transparency

If you want to punch a hole in an object, you need to use the Join Objects command. This command lets you have one object act as a see-through, or transparent hole, in another.

To use the Join command:

1. Select two or more objects.

2. Choose **Modify > Join**. The areas where the objects overlap are transparent **⑳**.

TIP Text characters that have two or more parts, such as the letters *D*, *B*, *o*, or *g* are automatically joined when you convert the text to paths (*see page 124*).

Objects that have been joined, can then be split apart.

To use the Split command:

1. Select the joined objects.

2. Choose **Modify > Split**. The areas where the objects overlap are no longer transparent.

TIP (Win) You can also use the Join and Split icons on the Modify toolbar to easily change objects.

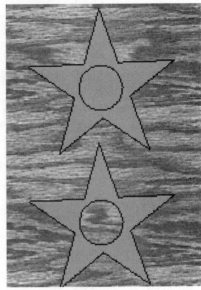

⑳ *Applying the* **Join** *command creates a hole where two objects overlap.*

Join Command; Split Command

Before

After

㉑ *The results of applying the* **Mask Group** *command. Note that the original brush stroke around the mask object is not visible.*

Masking is the technique of using the shape of one object as a contour to crop other objects. Only those parts of the objects that are within the mask are visible. Fireworks gives you two different ways of creating masks. The first way is to create a Mask Group.

To create a Mask Group:

1. Make sure the object that is to act as the mask is the topmost object.

2. Select the objects to be masked as well as the mask.

3. Choose **Modify**>**Mask Group**. The objects behind the mask are visible only within the fill area of the mask, the topmost object **㉑**.

TIP You cannot see the fill or brush stroke for an object that has been made into the mask of a mask group.

Before

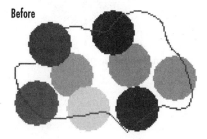

After

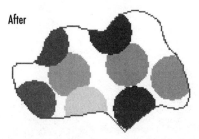

㉒ *The results of applying the* **Paste Inside** *command. Note that the brush stroke around the mask object is still visible.*

The other way to mask objects it to use the Paste Inside command.

To use Paste Inside to mask objects:

1. Position the objects to be masked on top of the object that is to act as the mask.

2. Cut the objects.

3. Select the object that is to act as the mask.

4. Choose **Edit**>**Paste Inside**. The objects appear within the fill of the mask **㉒**.

TIP You can see the fill or brush stroke for an object that has been made into a mask using Paste Inside.

Once you have created a mask, you may want to move the objects inside the mask. This technique works with either type of mask.

To move objects within a mask:

1. Select the mask with the Pointer tool. A small mask handle appears **㉓**.

2. Drag the mask handle. This moves the items within the mask.

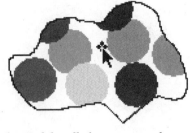

㉓ The **Mask handle** *lets you move the contents inside a mask.*

The Opacity panel also lets you change how the colors of one object interact with the colors of other objects below it. This is similar to the layer blending modes in Adobe Photoshop.

To change the object blending mode:

1. Select the top object you want to change.

2. Use the blending mode pop-up list to choose the blending mode for the object **㉔**.

㉔ The **Blending mode** *pop-up list*

For a color printout of the blending modes shown in figures ㉕–㊱, see the color insert.

The Normal blending mode

Choose **Normal** to have the object not interact with the objects below it.

The Multiply blending mode

Choose **Multiply** to add the colors of the object to the objects below **㉕**. This is similar to the results of overprinting one object over another.

㉕ *The results of the **Multiply** blending mode*

26 *The results of the* **Screen** *blending mode*

27 *The results of the* **Darken** *blending mode*

28 *The results of the* **Lighten** *blending mode*

29 *The results of the* **Difference** *blending mode*

The Screen blending mode

Choose **Screen** to subtract the colors of the object from the objects below **26**. This is similar to the results of bleaching out one image from the other.

The Darken blending mode

Choose **Darken** to have the colors of the object visible only where they are darker than the objects below **27**.

The Lighten blending mode

Choose **Lighten** to have the colors of the object visible only where they are lighter than the objects below **28**.

The Difference blending mode

Choose **Difference** to have the colors of the object create a difference between them and the objects below. If the colors are the same, the result is black. The greater the difference, the lighter the color **29**.

The Hue blending mode

Choose **Hue** to have the hue of the object applied onto the objects below without changing the brightness or saturation of the image ❸.

❸ *The results of the Hue blending mode*

The Saturation blending mode

Choose **Saturation** to have the saturation of the object applied onto the objects below without changing the hue or brightness ❸.

❸ *The results of the Saturation blending mode*

The Color blending mode

Choose **Color** to have the hue and saturation of the object applied onto the objects below without changing the brightness ❸.

❸ *The results of the Color blending mode*

The Luminosity blending mode

Choose **Luminosity** to have the lightness information of an object applied to the objects below without changing the hue, saturation, or brightness ❸.

❸ *The results of the Luminosity blending mode*

③④ *The results of the* **Invert** *blending mode*

③⑤ *The results of the* **Tint** *blending mode*

③⑥ *The results of the* **Erase** *blending mode*

The Invert blending mode

Choose **Invert** to have the shape of the top object reverse the colors of the objects below—for instance, black becomes white, green becomes red, blue becomes yellow. The color of the top object has no effect on the results of the Invert command **③④**.

The Tint blending mode

Choose **Tint** to have the color of the top object tint the objects below **③⑤**.

The Erase blending mode

Choose **Erase** to have the shape of the top object act like a mask on the objects below. Only objects outside the top object will be visible. The color of the top object has no effect on the results of the Erase command **③⑥**.

Invert; Tint; Erase

If you have created an object with a certain set of intricate fill settings—for instance a special gradient, feathering, and texture—it might be cumbersome to reapply all those settings to another object created later. Rather, you can copy the settings from one object to another ❸❼.

To paste attributes from one object to another:

1. Select the object with the attributes you want to copy.

2. Choose **Edit**>**Copy**.

3. Select the object with the attributes you want to change.

4. Choose **Edit**>**Paste Attributes**. The second object takes on all the settings of the first.

TIP Changes made using the Vector controls (*see page 86*) are not saved when copying and pasting attributes.

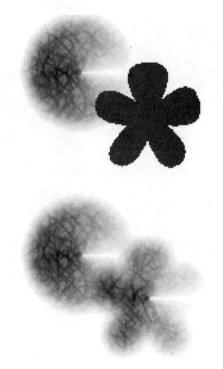

❸❼ *The results of applying the* **Paste Attributes** *command*

The other part of coloring vector objects in Fireworks is applying a brush. A brush is the color or effect applied along the path of an object. In ordinary vector-drawing programs, a brush is called a stroke. However, the effects in Fireworks created along paths are so sophisticated, and can resemble the looks of many different paint brushes, that it seems apt to call them brushes.

In this chapter you will learn how to

View the Brush panel.

Apply a basic brush.

Change the brush attributes.

Apply textures to a brush.

Use the Pencil tool.

Save brush settings.

Create a natural brush stroke.

Use the Path Scrubber tool.

Create your own brushes.

Change the position of a brush on a path.

Change how the fill reacts with a brush.

You control the look of brushes with the Brush panel. The brushes in the Brush panel can be applied to closed paths such as rectangles or to open paths such as those created by the Pen, Pencil, or Brush tools.

To view the Brush panel:

Choose **Window**>**Brush** to open the Brush panel **❶**.

or

Click the Brush panel tab to change from the Fill or Effects panel.

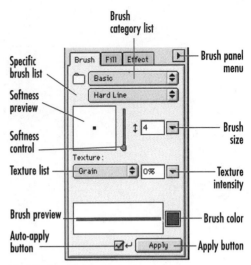

❶ *The* **Brush panel**

A brush in Fireworks can be a simple colored line resembling a pencil stroke, or it can be a multicolored paint splatter. The best way to understand brushes is to start with a basic brush and then work your way up to the more sophisticated effects.

To apply a basic brush:

1. Select the Brush tool in the Toolbox **❷**.
2. Select Basic from the brush category pop-up list.
3. Drag the Brush tool in the document area. A brush stroke appears along the path you just created.

❷ *The* **Brush tool** *in the Toolbox*

4. Click the button state box to set the Color Mixer to the brush mode.

TIP You can also use the buttons in the Color Mixer or the Toolbox to set the Color Mixer to the brush mode.

5. Use the Color Mixer to select a color. (*For more information on working with the Color Mixer, see Chapter 3, "Colors."*)

TIP When you create a path with the Brush or Pencil tools (*see pages 50 and 52*), the fill is automatically changed to none. This gives the look of a simple brush stroke, rather than a vector object.

Brush Panel; Basic Brush

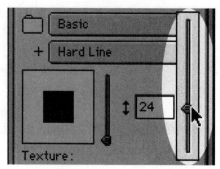

❸ *The* **Brush size** *slider*

❹ *The* **Brush softness** *slider*

The easiest way to understand brushes is to change the attributes of a selected path.

To change the brush attributes:

1. Start with the basic brush created in the previous exercise.

2. Drag the size slider or enter an amount in the field to change the size of the brush ❸.

3. Drag the softness slider to soften the edge along the brush stroke ❹.

TIP You may need to increase the size of the brush to see the difference in the edge softness.

4. Choose one of the preset brushes from the brush name pop-up list to change the shape of the brush.

TIP Each of the 11 brush categories has its own preset brushes making a total of 48 different brushes to choose from. (*For a printout of all the default brush categories, see Appendix A.*)

Brush Attributes

As with the textures for fills, you can apply textures to brushes.

To apply textures to a brush:

1. Choose one of the textures from the Texture pop-up list. (*For a complete printout of all the default textures, see Appendix A.*)

   TIP The texture for brushes are the same textures used for fills. However, a brush stroke can have a different texture than the fill for the object **❺**.

2. Use the slider or enter a number in the Intensity field to see the effects of the texture on the fill.

   TIP As with patterns, you can bring in textures from other applications to use within Fireworks (*see page 89*).

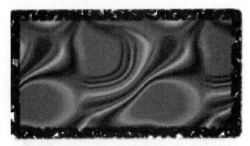

❺ *Two different textures applied to the brush and fill of an object.*

❻ *The Pencil tool in the Toolbox*

The Pencil tool creates paths like the Brush tool. However, the size and shape of the Pencil tool is set so that it automatically creates the thin lines of a pencil.

To use the Pencil tool:

1. Click the Pencil tool in the Toolbox **❻**.

2. Drag a path on the page. The Brush settings automatically change to the Pencil tool settings.

3. Choose one of the preset settings for the Pencil tool **❼**.

4. Drag to create the various Pencil paths.

   TIP When you select the Brush or the Pencil tools, any fill that was set in the Fill panel resets automatically to none.

   TIP Paths created by the Pencil tool can be changed by applying any of the brush categories.

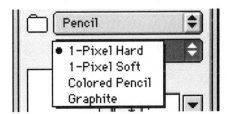

❼ *The Pencil tool presets*

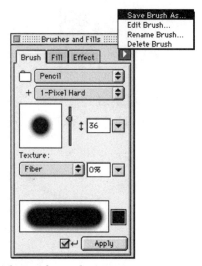

❽ *The* Brush panel *menu*

Any changes to the brush panel, such as the size, edge softness, or texture, are modifications of the brush preset. You can save those changes as your own brush preset.

To save brush panel settings:

1. Make whatever changes you want to the Brush setting. A plus appears next to the brush name indicating that the brush has been modified.

2. Choose Save Brush As from the Brush panel menu ❽. The Save Brush dialog box appears.

3. Type the name of the new brush and click OK. The new brush appears as one of the brush presets.

Pressure means more than just meeting tight deadlines. If you work with a pressure-sensitive tablet, you can easily see how responsive the Fireworks brushes are to changes in how you press with the stylus. However, even if you draw with a mouse, you can still make a more natural brush stroke based on how you drag with the mouse.

To create a natural brush stroke:

1. Select the Brush tool.

2. Choose a brush such as Airbrush set to Basic or Calligraphy set to Quill.

TIP These brushes respond very well to variations in mouse movements.

3. Drag along a path pausing without releasing the mouse button. The width of the brush stroke increases where you pause in the drag ❾.

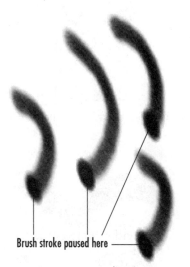

Brush stroke paused here

❾ *The effect of pausing while creating four brush strokes.*

You can also alter the look of the brush after it has been applied to a path by using the Path Scrubber tool. This tool allows you to increase or decrease the pressure on a path. The Path Scrubber has two modes: Path Scrubber Plus and Path Scrubber Minus.

TIP If you have a pressure-sensitive tablet, the Path Scrubber can be used to further refine the look of the path. If you do not have a pressure-sensitive pen and tablet, you can use the Path Scrubber to simulate those effects.

To use the Path Scrubber tool:

1. Select a path with a brush stroke.
2. Choose the Path Scrubber Plus tool in the Toolbox ❿. (If you do not see the Path Scrubber Plus tool, press the pop-up group to select the tool.)
3. Drag along the path. The width of the stroke increases as you drag ⓫.
4. Choose the Path Scrubber Minus tool in the Toolbox ⓬.
5. Drag across the path. The width of the stroke decreases as you drag ⓭.

TIP Hold the Option/Alt key to switch between the Path Scrubber Plus and Minus modes.

❿ *The* **Path Scrubber Plus tool** *in the Toolbox*

⓫ *The effects of the Path Scrubber Plus tool on a brush stroke*

⓬ *The* **Path Scrubber Minus tool** *in the Toolbox*

⓭ *The effects of the Path Scrubber Minus tool*

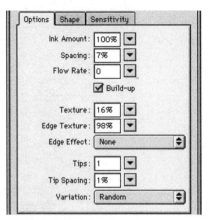

⓮ *The* **Brush Options** *dialog box*

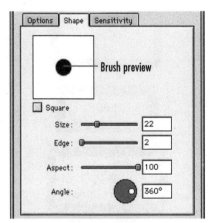

⓯ *The* **Brush Shape** *dialog box*

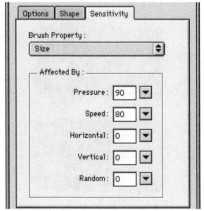

⓰ *The* **Brush Sensitivity** *dialog box*

In addition to the settings in the Brush panel, there are more controls that control the appearance of brush strokes. You do not have to open these settings to use Fireworks. However, as you become more comfortable with Fireworks, you may want to experiment with these controls.

To create your own brushes:

1. Choose Edit Brush from the Brush panel menu. The Edit Brush dialog box appears.
2. Click the tab for Options to control the appearance of the brush ⓮.
3. Click the tab for Shape to control the size, edge softness, shape, roundness, and angle of the brush ⓯.

TIP You can override the settings for size by changing the size and edge in the main Brush panel.

4. Click the tab for Sensitivity to control how the brush reacts to changes in the mouse or stylus movements ⓰.

Create Your Own Brushes

Unlike other vector programs, Fireworks gives you a choice as to where a brush is displayed on a path.

To change the position of a brush on a path:

1. Select the path.

2. Choose **Modify**>**Object Properties** to open the Object Properties dialog box **❼**.

3. Use the pop-up list to choose between Centered, Inside or Outside to change the position of the brush along the path **❽**.

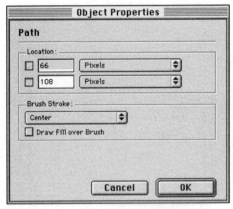

❼ *The* **Object Properties** *dialog box*

When a path has both a brush and a fill, you have a choice as to how the fill interacts over the brush.

To change how the fill reacts with a brush:

1. Select the path.

2. Choose **Modify**>**Object Properties** to open the Object Properties dialog box.

3. Check Draw Fill Over Brush to have the fill of the object extend over the path **❽**.

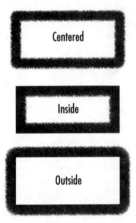

❽ *The three choices for the* **position of a brush on a path**

❾ *The effects of changing the* **Draw Fill Over Brush** *setting*

EFFECTS 9

Beyond fills and brushes, Fireworks lets you add an effect to objects. These effects serve two different purposes. First, they lets you create special effects such as shadows, glows, and bevels. Second, they provide the different looks for rollover buttons. (*For more information on creating rollover buttons, see Chapter 17, "Slices."*)

Unlike the effects created in pixel-based programs, the effects in Fireworks can be edited at any time. This means that you can apply an effect and then change it later.

In this chapter you will learn how to:

View the Effect panel.

Apply an Inner or Outer Bevel effect.

Change the color of an Outer Bevel.

Use the Button state controls.

Apply a Drop Shadow effect.

Apply an Emboss effect.

Apply a Glow effect.

Save an effect.

Apply multiple effects.

Any object—path, text, or image—can have an effect applied to it.

To view the Effect panel:

1. Choose **Window** > **Effect** to open the Effect panel.

   or

   Click the Effect panel tab to change from the Fill or Brush panel.

   TIP If you make changes to the Effect panel, you can save those changes as new preset effects (*see page 111*).

❶ *Different looks that can be created using the* **Inner and Outer Bevel effects**

The two most interesting effects are the Inner and Outer Bevel effects ❶.

To apply a bevel effect:

1. Select the object.

2. Choose Inner Bevel or Outer Bevels from the Effect category pop-up list. The Effect panel changes to show the bevel choices ❷.

3. Choose one of the Effect presets from the Effect name pop-up list ❸. (*For a complete printout of all the default effect presets, see Appendix A.*)

4. Press the Size control to open the slider or type in the field to change the size of the bevel.

5. Press the Contrast control to open the slider or type in the field to change the intensity of the light creating the bevel highlights and shadows.

6. Press the Softness control to open the slider or type in the field to change the hardness of the edges of the bevel.

   TIP If the bevel around curved objects appears appears bumpy, increase the softness to smooth the bevel.

7. Use the Lighting wheel or type in the field to change the angle of the light.

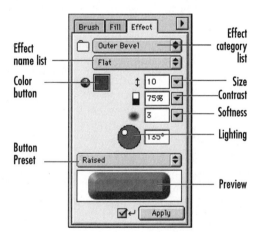

Effect name list
Color button
Button Preset

Effect category list
Size
Contrast
Softness
Lighting
Preview

❷ *The* **Bevel effects** *panel*

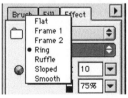

❸ *The* **Bevel preset** *choices*

Effect Panel; Bevels

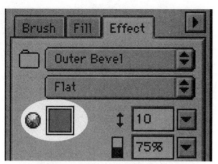

❹ *The* **Color button** *for the Effects panel*

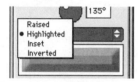

❺ *The* **Bevel Preset** *list*

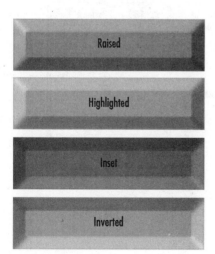

❻ *The effects of* applying the Bevel Preset choices

The color of an Inner Bevel comes from the color of the original object. The color of an Outer Bevel can be changed using the Effect panel.

To change the color of a bevel:

1. Click the color button in the Effect panel ❹.

2. Use the Color Mixer to set the color.

TIP You can also double-click the color button to open the color mixer.

Using the Bevel Presets.

The Bevel Preset pop-up list for the bevel effects is used to easily apply variations to the bevels. The four states are Raised, Highlighted, Inset, and Inverted ❺.

TIP The Bevel Preset are a simply a convenience for creating rollover buttons. They do not actually apply the JavaScript code for rollovers.

The four presets change the appearance of the bevels as follows ❻:

• **Raised** leaves the object as originally styled.

• **Highlighted** lightens the object as if a 25% white tint were applied over it.

• **Inset** reverses the lighting of the bevel to invert the 3-D effect.

• **Inverted** reverses the lighting and lightens the object with a tint.

TIP Any type of object can be used as a rollover; not just the objects with bevels applied to them.

(*For more information on creating rollover buttons, see Chapter 18, "Rollovers."*)

In addition to the bevels, there are three other effects you can apply to objects. The first of these effect is a Drop Shadow ❼.

To apply a Drop Shadow effect:

1. Chose Drop Shadow from the Effect category list. The Effect panel changes to show the shadow choices ❽.

2. Choose one of the Drop Shadow presets from the Effect names list.

3. Press the Opacity control to open the slider or type a number in the field to change the transparency of the shadow. The lower the number the more transparent the object.

4. Press the Softness control to open the slider or type a number in the field to change the softness or feather applied to the edge of the shadow.

5. Use the Lighting wheel or type in the field to change the angle of the light casting the shadow.

6. Press the Distance control to open the slider or type a number in the field to change how far the shadow appears from the object.

7. Click the color button and then use the Color Mixer to change the color of the shadow.

TIP The color of the shadow changes when the opacity of the shadow is increased or decreased.

8. Select Knock Out to have only the shadow appear, not the object casting the shadow.

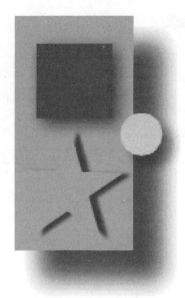

❼ *Different looks that can be created using the* **Drop Shadow** *effect*

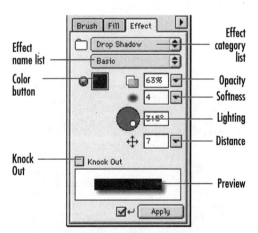

❽ *The* **Drop Shadow effects** *panel*

Effect category list
Effect name list
Color button
Opacity
Softness
Lighting
Distance
Knock Out
Preview

Drop Shadow
Basic
63%
4
315°
7
Knock Out
Apply

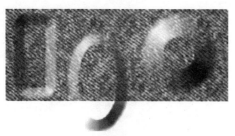

❾ *Different looks that can be created using the* **Emboss** *effect*

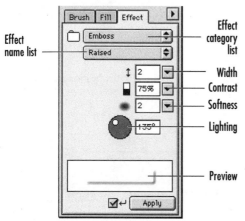

❿ *The* **Emboss** *effects panel*

Effect name list

Brush | Fill | Effect

Emboss

Raised

Effect category list

Width
Contrast
Softness
Lighting

Preview

Apply

⓫ *Embossed objects take their color from the objects behind them.*

The next effect is Emboss. This pushes the shape of one object into the background or into other objects **❾**.

To apply an Emboss effect:

1. Choose Emboss from the Effect category list. The Effect panel changes to show the emboss effect choices **❿**.

2. Choose one of the Emboss presets from the Effect names pop-up list.

3. Use the Width slider or type a number in the field to change the width or size of the embossing.

4. Use the Contrast slider or type a number in the field to change the intensity of the light creating the embossing highlights and shadows.

5. Use the Softness slider or type a number in the field to change the hardness of the edges of the embossing.

6. Use the Lighting wheel or type a number in the field to change the angle of the light on the embossing.

To change the appearance of the embossing:

Embossing always takes its appearance from the object it is over, the canvas color of the document, or any image on the background layer **⓫**. You control the look of embossing by changing the color of the object, canvas (*see page 21*) or the image on the background (*see Chapter 11, "Pixel Images"*).

Embossing: Embossing Color

The Glow effect lets you add a color all around the edges of an object **⑫**.

To apply a Glow effect:

1. Choose Glow from the Effect category pop-up list. The Glow effect choices appear **⑬**.

2. Press the Opacity control to open the slider or type a number in the field to change the transparency of the glow. The lower the number, the greater the transparency.

3. Press the Softness control to open the slider or type a number in the field to change the softness, or feather, applied to the glow.

4. Press the Width control to open the slider or type a number in the field to change the size of the glow.

5. Click the color button and then use the Color Mixer to change the color of the glow.

⑫ *Different looks that can be created using the* **Glow** *effect*

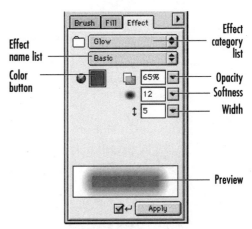

⑬ *The* **Glow** *effects panel*

Effect name list

Color button

Effect category list

Opacity
Softness
Width

Preview

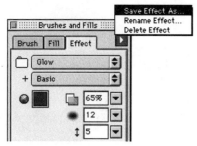

⑭ *The* Effect panel menu

Every time you change the choices for an effect, you create a new effect. You can save those choices for use on other objects or in other documents.

To save an effect:

1. Make whatever changes you want to the effect. A plus appears next to the effect name indicating that the effect has been modified.

2. Choose Save Effect As from the Effect panel menu **⑭**. The Save Effect dialog box appears.

3. Type the name of the new effect and click OK. The new effect appears as one of the effect presets.

TIP The settings created for an effect are specific to that effect category. So the settings for an Inner Bevel do not appear when the Outer Bevel is chosen.

Once you apply one effect to an object, you may want to apply another effect. You use the group command to add other effects to an object.

To apply multiple effects:

1. Apply the first effect to the object.

2. Choose **Modify > Group**. The group object handles appear around the object.

3. Use the Effect category pop-up list to apply the second effect to the object.

4. Group the object again to apply other effects.

TIP The order that you apply multiple effects is important **16**. For instance, if you apply an outer bevel first, and then a drop shadow, the shadow is created from the entire object, including the outer bevel area. If you reverse the order, the bevel is created underneath the area of the shadow.

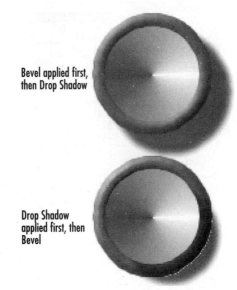

Bevel applied first, then Drop Shadow

Drop Shadow applied first, then Bevel

16 *The order in which effects are applied changes the final result.*

Palettes

The illustrations below show three of the most important preset Swatches palettes.

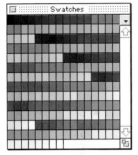

The **216 Web-safe colors** Swatches panel discussed on page 35

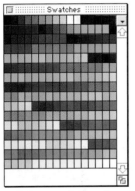

The **Macintosh System Colors** Swatches panel discussed on page 35

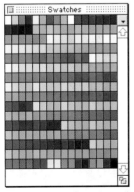

The **Windows System Colors** Swatches panel discussed on page 36

Adaptive Palettes

The illustrations below show the results of the adaptive palettes settings described on pages 166–167.

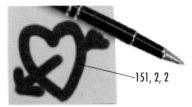

The original Fireworks file had the heart painted with an RGB color.

Using the Adobe Photoshop Adaptive settings to change the file to Index color shifts the color to a different RGB value.

Using the Fireworks Adaptive settings maintains the RGB values.

Using the Fireworks Web-snap Adaptive settings shifts the RGB color to a Web-safe color. This leaves the color flat when viewed by 8-bit monitors.

Adaptive color file sizes

The illustrations below show how exporting as a GIF with an Adaptive palette shrinks the file size significantly: the lower the number of colors, the lower the file size. For more information on exporting as GIF images, see pages 164–167.

All the colors of the original image are maintained when exported with the **Adaptive palette using 256 colors** *(8.01 K).*

A small number of colors are changed when exported with the **Adaptive palette using 64 colors** *(5.35 K).*

Even more colors are noticeably changed when exported with the **Adaptive palette using 8 colors** *(3.58 K).*

Web palette or Adpative palette

The illustrations below show the effects of exporting using the Adaptive palette or using a Web palette with or without dithering. For more information on exporting as GIF images, see pages 164–167.

The **Adaptive palette** *maintains as many of the original colors as possible. Notice the subtle shade for the face and hands.*

The **Web 216 palette with dithering on** *creates a pattern of dots in the shirt, face and hands to simulate non-Web colors. This is unacceptable for flat art.*

The **Web 216 palette with dithering off** *shifts the colors in the shirt, face, and hands to the closest Web-safe color.*

JPEG or GIF Comparisons

The illustrations below show how much better JPEG images are in maintaining the tones of an image than GIF files. For more information on exporting as JPEG images, see pages 164–169.

JPEG Comparisons

The illustrations below show the effects of exporting with different JPEG settings. Notice how the quality of the image degrades only slightly while the file size is reduced greatly. Notice also the effects of smoothing. For more information on exporting as JPEG images, see pages 164–169.

GIF Web 216 dithered with 88 colors *(37.7 K)*

JPEG at 100% quality *(100.81K)*

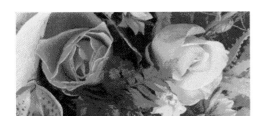

GIF Adaptive dithered with 64 colors *(38.67 K)*

JPEG at 70% quality *(17.58 K)*

JPEG at 90% quality *(29.4 K)*

JPEG at 30% quality *(10.01 K)*

JPEG at 70% quality *(15.98 K)*

JPEG at 30% quality, smoothing of 2 *(9.26 K)*

The Default Gradient Colors

For more information on working with gradients, see pages 83–86.

The **Black, White** *gradient*

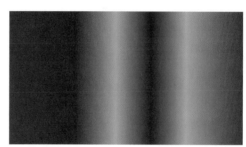

The **Cobalt Blue** *gradient*

The **Blue, Red, Yellow** *gradient*

The **Copper** *gradient*

The **Blue, Yellow, Blue** *gradient*

The **Emerald Green** *gradient*

The **Pastels** *gradient*

The **Silver** *gradient*

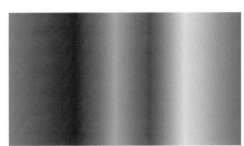

The **Red, Blue** *gradient*

The **Spectrum** *gradient*

The **Red, Green, Blue** *gradient*

The **Violet, Orange** *gradient*

The Blending Modes

For a detailed explanation of these modes, see pages 92–95.

*The **Normal** blending mode*

*The **Darken** blending mode*

*The **Multiply** blending mode*

*The **Lighten** blending mode*

*The **Screen** blending mode*

*The **Difference** blending mode*

*The **Hue** blending mode*

*The **Invert** blending mode*

*The **Saturation** blending mode*

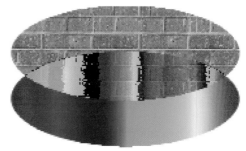

*The **Tint** blending mode*

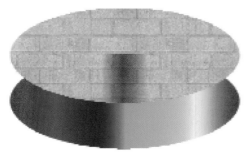

*The **Color** blending mode*

*The **Erase** blending mode*

*The **Luminosity** blending mode*

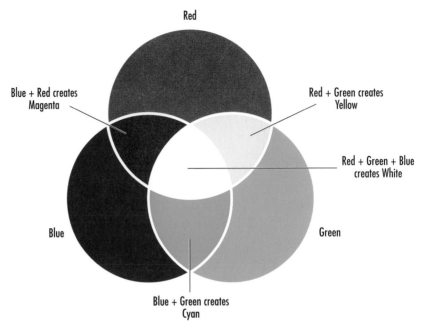

Red

Blue + Red creates
Magenta

Red + Green creates
Yellow

Red + Green + Blue
creates White

Blue

Green

Blue + Green creates
Cyan

An example of **additive colors**, *sometimes called RGB (For more information see page 30.)*

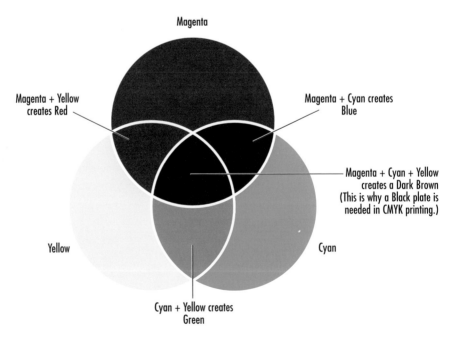

Magenta

Magenta + Yellow
creates Red

Magenta + Cyan creates
Blue

Magenta + Cyan + Yellow
creates a Dark Brown
(This is why a Black plate is
needed in CMYK printing.)

Yellow

Cyan

Cyan + Yellow creates
Green

An example of **subtractive colors**, *sometimes called process colors (For more information see page 32.)*

Whoever said a picture is worth a thousand words underestimated by several hundred kilobytes. Pictures, or graphics, create much bigger Web files than text. So why convert fast-moving text into slow-moving graphics? It might be to create labels, create a banner design, or just make sure the text looks the same no matter what fonts or system the viewer has. Whatever the reason, Fireworks has many features for working with text.

In this chapter you will learn how to

Use the Text tool.

Open the Text Editor.

Set the font and point size.

Add electronic styling.

Kern text.

Set the range kerning.

Set the horizontal scale.

Set the leading.

Add a baseline shift.

Set the horizontal text alignment.

Set the vertical text alignment.

Reverse the text flow.

Modify text inside a text block.

Open the Text Editor for a text block.

Transform text in a text block.

Set the object properties for a text block.

Attach text to a path.

To change the position and orientation of the text.

To reverse the direction of the text.

Apply path attributes to text.

Convert text to paths.

You access text in Fireworks by using the Text tool. You should find working with text similar to the methods you have used in any graphics or page-layout program.

To use the Text tool:

1. Choose the Text tool in the Toolbox ❶.

2. Click inside the document area or drag to create the area that you want the text to stay inside. This opens the Text Editor ❷.

TIP If you click with the Text tool, the text box starts at that spot and extends to the edge of the document area.

❶ *The* **Text tool** *in the Toolbox*

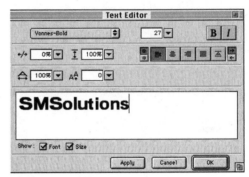

❷ *The* **Text Editor**

In addition to the formatting controls, there are a few special controls you can use inside the Text Editor.

To use the Text Editor:

1. Type the text inside the Preview area.

2. Use any of the ordinary text techniques to select text, make corrections, or insert new text within the Preview area.

3. Click Font and Size to see the Text as it will appear in the document.

TIP Turn off the Font and Size display if you find it difficult to read the text within the Text Editor.

4. Click Apply to see the formatting changes without leaving the Text Editor.

5. Click OK to close the Text Editor.

❸ *The **font list** in the Text Editor*

❹ *The **point size** control in the Text Editor*

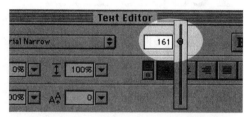

❺ *The **styling** controls in the Text Editor*

To set the font:

1. Use the font pop-up list ❸ to choose the typeface. Then type the text inside the Preview area.

2. Use the font pop-up list to change to a different typeface.

TIP Fireworks allows you to mix different typefaces within the Preview area.

To set the point size:

Use the point size slider or type in the field ❹ to change the point size.

Fireworks also lets you add bold or italic styling to text.

To add electronic styling:

1. Select the text.

2. Click the bold or italic buttons to change text ❺.

TIP The electronic styling applied in Fireworks is not the actual bold or italic typeface. It is an electronic simulation of bold or italic text. However, it does export as part of the finished graphic.

TIP Electronic styling is discarded when text is converted into paths (*see page 124*).

Font; Point Size; Electronic Styling

Kerning is adjusting the space between two letters. Fireworks lets you kern text within the Text Editor.

To kern the text:

1. Click between the two letters you want to kern.

2. Use the Kern slider or type in the field ❻ to kern the text closer together or further apart. Negative values decrease the space; positive values increase the space ❼.

TIP The Preview does not show the effects of kerning. To see those effects, position the Text Editor outside the document area and then use the Apply button to see the changes as you enter the kerning amounts.

❻ *The* **kerning** *controls in the Text Editor*

People Inc.
People Inc.

❼ *The result of kerning between the letters* **Pe**, **pl**, *and* **le**

Range kerning is kerning applied to a selection of text. (Range kerning is sometimes called *tracking* in other programs.)

To set the range kerning:

1. Drag across a selection of the text.

2. Use the Range Kerning slider or type in the field to change the range kerning for the text ❽. Negative values decrease the space; positive values increase the space ❾.

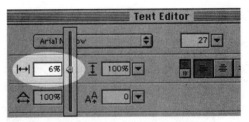

❽ *The* **range kerning** *controls in the Text Editor*

People Inc.
People Inc.

❾ *The results of applying range kerning to the text*

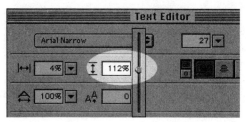

⑩ *The leading controls in the Text Editor*

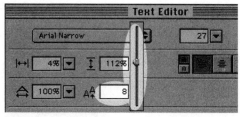

⑪ *The baseline shift controls in the Text Editor*

People Inc.
People Inc.

⑫ *The results of apply a positive baseline shift to the characters nc. (The baseline is indicated by the dashed line.)*

Leading, or *linespacing*, is the space between multiple lines of text. If your text is only on a single line, you do not have to worry about setting leading.

To set the leading:

Use the Leading slider or type in the field to change the leading for the text **⑩**.

TIP Fireworks measures leading as a percentage of the point size. 100% means the leading is the same as the point size.

TIP Leading is applied to an entire paragraph, not individual characters.

Baseline shift is the technique of raising or lowering text from its *baseline*, or the line that the text sits on.

To add a baseline shift:

1. Select the text.
2. Use the baseline slider or type in the field **⑪** to raise or lower the text in points from the baseline.

TIP Positive numbers raise the text. Negative numbers lower the text **⑫**.

Text can also be distorted using a techniques called horizontal scaling. This changes the width of the text without changing the height.

To change the horizontal scale:

1. Select the text.

2. Use the horizontal scale slider or type in the field ⓭ to increase or decrease the horizontal scaling. Amounts lower than 100% make the text width smaller. Amounts higher than 100% make the text wider.

TIP Typography purists (such as this author) disdain the look of electronically scaled type ⓮. They say it causes ugly distortions to the look of the original typeface.

They also say that if you need to fit text into a specific area you should use the proper condensed or expanded typeface. However, even the purists cannot always tell if small amounts of scaling have been applied.

Text can also be set with a wide variety of alignment options. The text can be set either horizontally or vertically. Horizontal text reads from left to right.

To set the horizontal alignment:

1. Select the text.

2. Click one of the five horizontal alignment settings: left, right, centered, justified, or stretched alignment ⓯.

TIP Justified alignment increases the range kerning so the line fills the width of the text block ⓰.

TIP Stretched alignment distorts the shape of the text as it increases the horizontal scale so the line fills the width of the text block ⓱. This could cause typography purists to cringe (*see tip in previous exercise*).

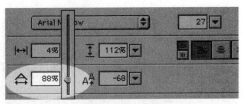

⓭ *The horizontal scale controls in the Text Editor*

People Inc.
People Inc.

⓮ *The results of applying horizontal scale to the letter* **P**

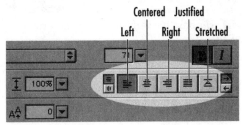

⓯ *The alignment controls in the Text Editor*

> People Inc.
> People Inc.

⓰ *The results of applying the justified alignment*

> People Inc.
> People Inc.

⓱ *The results of applying the stretch alignment*

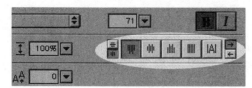

⓲ *The* **vertical alignment** *controls*

⓳ *The* **reverse text** *controls*

S M S C
C S M S

⓴ **Text reversed** *to read from right to left*

Text can also be set so it reads from top to bottom. This is very useful for creating vertical buttons.

To set the vertical alignment:

1. Select the text.

2. Click the vertical alignment button **⓲** to access the five vertical alignment settings: top, bottom, centered, justified, or stretched alignment.

TIP Vertical alignment does not show in the Text Editor. Use the Apply button to see the actual vertical alignment.

Another special effect you can create with text is to have the text read from right to left. This can also be useful when working with certain foreign typefaces.

To reverse the text flow:

Click the right-to-left button **⓳**. All the text in that text block changes so that the letters flow from right to left **⓴**.

Once text is in a text block, you do not have to open the Text Editor to make certain formatting changes.

To modify text inside a text block:

1. Drag any of the text block handles to rewrap the text within the block ㉑.

2. Choose **Text** > **Font** to change the typeface.

3. Choose **Text** > **Size** to change the point size.

4. Choose **Text** > **Style** to apply one of the electronic styles.

5. Choose **Text** > **Alignment** to apply any of the horizontal or vertical alignment settings.

TIP Changes applied from the Text menu are applied to all the text within the text block. You cannot apply the changes to just some of the text.

㉑ **Drag the text block handles** *to change the way the text wraps within the block.*

To reopen the Text Editor:

Choose **Text** > **Editor**.

or

Double-click the text block.

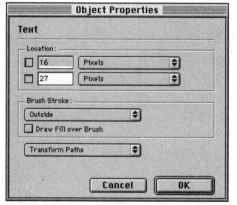

㉒ *The results of applying a distortion to the text within a text block*

You can use the transformation tools on text with some spectacular results.

To transform text in a text block:

1. Select the text block.

2. Use any of the the Transform tools (*see pages 67–71*) to distort the text within the block **㉒**.

TIP The transformation tools change the size of the text by distorting the text, not by changing the point size.

TIP Choose **Modify>Transform>Remove Transformations** to restore the text to its original formatting.

㉓ *The* **Object Properties** *dialog box for a text block*

When you distort text, you have a choice as to how the text is distorted. This is controlled by the object properties for text.

To set the object properties for a text block:

1. Select the text block.

2. Choose **Modify>Object Properties** to open the Object Properties dialog box for a text block **㉓**.

3. Choose Transform Paths or Transform Pixels.

TIP Transform Paths results in distortions that preserve crisp text. Transform Pixels results in distortions in which the text may be blurred.

One of the most popular effects in graphics is to attach text so it flows along a path.

To attach text to a path:

1. Select the text block.

2. Select the path.

3. Choose **Text**>**Attach to Path**. The text automatically aligns to the path ❷❹.

TIP Text attached to a path can still be edited using the Text Editor (*see page 114*).

❷❹ *The results of* attaching text to a path

Once you have text on a path, you can change the alignment, or the position where the text appears on the path.

To change the alignment of text on a path:

Choose **Text**>**Align** and then choose one of the alignment settings. This changes where the text is positioned ❷❺.

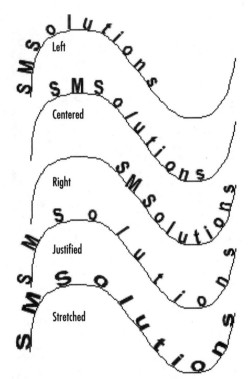

❷❺ *The results of* applying the different alignment settings *to text on a path*

26 *The Object Properties dialog box for* **text attached to a path**

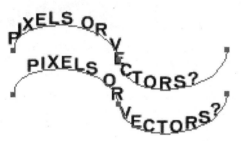

27 *The effects of adding a 20 pixel* **text offset** *to shift the text along a path*

Rotate Around
Path

Vertical

Skew Vertical

Skew Horizontal

28 *The results of applying the* **different orientation settings** *to text on a path*

You can also control where the text is positioned along the path. This is called the text offset.

To change the text offset along a path:

1. Select the text that has been attached to the path.

2. Choose **Modify>Object Properties** to open the Object properties dialog box **26**.

3. Change the amount in the Offset field and then click Apply or OK. The text moves along the path **27**.

You can also change how the individual characters of the text are positioned in relation to the angle of the path. This is called the *orientation* of the text.

To change the orientation of the text:

Choose **Text>Orientation** and then choose one of the orientation settings to change how the text is positioned on the path **28**.

- **Rotate Around Path** has the text keep a perpendicular orientation as it moves around the path.

- **Vectical** makes each character stand up straight no matter how the path curves.

- **Skew Vertical** maintains a vertical rotation but distorts the characters' shapes as the text follows the path.

- **Skew Horizontal** exaggerates the text's horizontal tilt up to a 90° rotation and distorts the characters' shapes as the text follows the path.

You can also reverse the direction of the path. This causes the text to flip to the other side of the path.

To reverse the direction of the text:

Choose **Text** > **Reverse Direction** to flip the text so that it flows on the other side of the path **29**.

29 *The results of applying the* **Reverse Direction** *command settings to text on a path*

You can apply any of the path attributes—fills, brushes, or effects—to text **30**.

To apply path attributes to text:

1. Select the text block or text on a path.
2. Use any of the Fill settings to change the inside of the text.
3. Use any of the Brush settings to add a stroke around the edge of the text.
4. Use any of the Effect settings to add effects to the text.

30 *The results of* **applying various fill, brush, and effect settings** *to text*

The text in a text block or attached to a path is called editable text. This means that you can work with the text—change the font or the letters—at any time. However, there are some effects you might want to create that require that the text be converted into paths.

To convert text to paths:

1. Select the text block or text on a path.
2. Choose **Text** > **Convert to Paths**. This converts the text into grouped paths.
3. Use any of the path selection tools to manipulate the paths **31**.

TIP Once you convert text to paths, you can no longer edit it in the Text Editor; you can edit it only as path objects then.

People Inc.
People Inc.

31 *The results of* **converting text to paths** *and then manipulating the converted paths*

PIXEL IMAGES 11

I t is the vector objects in Fireworks that make it so easy to use. But what if you want to use images such as photographs or scanned art that cannot be created by vector objects? Fortunately there is an alter ego to the vector side of Fireworks—a complete set of features for creating, importing, and working with pixel-based artwork. Technically the correct term for these graphics is pixel-based images. However, it is easier to call them *image objects* to differentiate them from the vector objects covered previously.

In this chapter you will learn how to

Access the background image.

Open scanned images.

Import scanned images.

Access the image-editing mode.

Combine or convert object.

Drop objects onto the background.

Flatten all the layers of the document.

Create an empty image.

macromedia
FIREWORKS

At the back of every Fireworks document is a background image. This is a pixel-based layer that provides the canvas over which all the other layers appear. While the original canvas color is set when a new document is opened, you can easily change that background image.

To access the background image:

Choose **Modify** > **Background Image**. This opens the background image in an image editing mode indicated by the thick black line around the image ❶.

or

Click the Background layer in the Layers panel. A square black dot indicates that the layer is active ❷ and that you are in the image editing mode.

TIP Once you have accessed the background image, you can paint on the image as you would in an ordinary paint program. (*To use the painting and selection tools in Fireworks, see Chapter 12, "Pixel Tools."*)

TIP To return to the object mode, click one of the regular layers or choose **Modify** > **Exit Image Edit**.

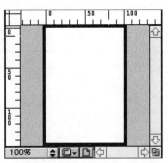

❶ *The black line indicates the background layer is in the* **Image Edit** *mode.*

❷ *When the background layer is selected it is in the* **Image Edit** *mode.*

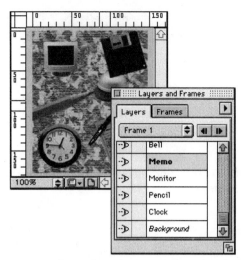

❸ Layers from Photoshop *are imported with the objects on their own Fireworks layers.*

When you create a new Fireworks document, the background is a single color that comes from the canvas color (*see page 21*). However, you can also bring in scanned artwork like photographs as the background canvas.

To open scanned images:

Choose **File > Open** and then find the file you want to open. Fireworks can open the following file formats: Adobe Photoshop 4 native file, TIFF, JPEG, GIF, BMP, PICT (Mac only), PNG, and Targa.

TIP The layers of Photoshop files are imported onto their own Fireworks layers ❸.

❹ *The **corner symbol** for imported artwork*

You can also import pixel-based images onto one of the object layers in Fireworks. This allows you to apply effects to the image object.

To import scanned images:

1. Choose **File > Import** and then find the file you want to import. Click OK. A small corner symbol ❹ indicates the file is ready for placing on the currently selected Fireworks layer.

2. Drag the corner symbol to draw a rectangle that the image scales to fit ❺.

   or

   Click to simply place the image at the original size.

❺ *Dragging the corner symbol places the imported artwork at a specific size.*

Once you have an imported image, you can switch to the image-editing mode to make changes to the pixels within the image.

To access the image-editing mode:

1. Select the image object that you want to edit.

2. Choose **Modify** > **Image Object**. A thick black line appears around the image indicating you can edit it **⊙**.

   or

   Double-click with the Pointer tool on the image object. This switches to the image-editing mode.

TIP To return to the object mode, deselect the object or choose **Modify** > **Exit Image Edit**.

⊙ *The* **thick line** *indicates that the image can be edited.*

If you have placed image objects in your Fireworks files, you may want to crop those images so they take up less space in your file.

To crop image objects:

1. Select the object you want to crop.

2. Choose **Edit** > **Crop Selected Image**. A set of handles appears around the image **⊙**.

3. Drag the handles so that they surround the area you want to keep.

4. When you have defined the area you want, double-click inside the handles. The excess image is deleted.

⊙ *The* **Crop handles** *let you discard portions of imported images.*

❽ *Two imported images can be moved or manipulated as separate images.*

❾ *The* **Convert to Image** *command merges the two imported images into one image object.*

You can also combine imported images, turn vector objects into image objects or add vector objects to image objects.

To combine or convert objects:

1. Select the objects you want to combine or convert **❽**.

2. Choose **Select** > **Convert to Image**. Imported images are combined into one image object **❾**.

TIP If you convert vector objects into image objects, you lose the ability to edit the paths surrounding an image.

Vector or image objects can be dropped onto the background layer. This converts the paths into pixels. Since the background layer is used for all the frames of a document, sending images to the background can be helpful in creating animations with a consistent background. (*For more information on creating animations, see Chapter 19, "Animations."*)

To drop objects onto the background:

1. Select the vector or image objects you want to put on the background.

2. Choose Drop Selection. This converts any vector objects to pixels and sends all the selected objects to the background.

TIP Choose **Select** > **Flatten Layers** to send all the objects on all the layers to the background and delete all but the background and foreground layers.

Image objects do not have to be filled with pixels. You can also create an empty image, which acts like a transparent image area. You can then paint or fill the transparent area using any of the image object tools.

To create an empty image:

1. Choose **Edit >Create Empty Image**. The cursor changes to a crosshair.

2. Drag with the crosshair to set the size of the empty image. The empty image is automatically selected in the image editing mode.

3. Use whichever tools you want to fill the empty image ❿.

❿ An **Empty Image** *allows you to use any of the image editing tools to paint inside the area.*

PIXEL TOOLS

Once you are in the Image Edit mode, many of the Fireworks tools change from path creation to pixel coloring. Tools reserved for image editing are now available in the Toolbox. If you have worked with paint programs such as Adobe Photoshop, Fractal Painter, MacPaint or Microsoft Paint, you will find it easy to work with the pixel tools in Fireworks.

In this chapter you will learn how to

Use the Marquee tools.

Use the Lasso tools.

Use the Magic Wand.

Use modifier keys to change the shape of selections.

Use the Selection commands.

Use the Similar command.

Use the Feather command.

Use the Rubber Stamp tool.

Use the Eraser.

Use the Eyedropper.

Use the Paint Bucket.

TIP Unless specified, all the exercises in this chapter assume that you are in one of the image-editing modes—working on the background layer, an imported image, or an image object. (*See Chapter 11, "Pixel Images."*)

Unlike vector objects, which are selected as paths, the pixels that make up image objects are selected as areas of the image. Several different tools select the areas of an image. The two basic selection tools are the marquee tools.

To use the Marquee tools:

1. Press the Marquee tool in the Toolbox and choose either the rectangular or elliptical shape ❶.

2. Move the cursor over the image area and drag diagonally to create a selection. A series of moving dashed lines (sometimes called *marching ants*) indicates the selected area ❷.

TIP Hold the Option/Alt key to draw the selection from the center outward.

TIP Hold the Shift key to constrain the selection to a square or circle.

3. Position the cursor inside the selection and drag to move that portion of the image to a new area.

4. Click outside the selection to deselect the marquee.

    or

    Choose **Select > None**.

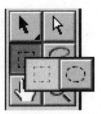

❶ *The* **Marquee tools** *in the Toolbox*

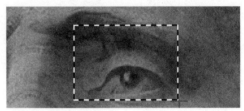

❷ *The* **marching ants** *of the marquee surround the selected area.*

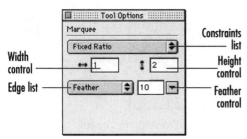

③ *The* **Marquee Tool Options** *panel*

The marquee tool *constraints* allow you to change the tool so that the area selected is a certain size or proportion.

To change the Marquee tool constraints:

1. Double-click either of the marquee tools in the Toolbox to open the Marquee Tool Options panel **③**.

2. Press the Constraints pop-up list to choose Normal, Fixed Ratio, or Fixed Size.

3. In the Fixed Ratio mode, enter the ratio for the width and the height of the selection. This constrains the marquee to those proportions.

4. In the Fixed Size mode, enter the pixel amounts for the width and height of the selection. This constrains the marquee area to that size.

④ *The* **Edge list** *choices*

You can also change the appearance of the edges of a marquee selection.

To change the Marquee tool edges:

1. In the Marquee Tool Options panel, press the edge list to choose Hard Edge, Anti-Alias, or Feather **④**.

   • Choose Hard Edge to give the selection a jagged edge **⑤**.

   • Choose Anti-Alias to give the selection a smoother edge **⑤**.

   • Choose Feather to blur the edges of the selection **⑤**.

2. If you choose the Feather, set the amount of the blur with the feather control slider or type the amount of the feather (in pixels) in the field.

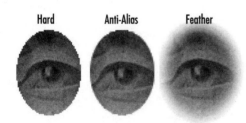

⑤ *The effects of* **changing the edge choices** *of a selection*

You might want to select shapes besides rectangles and ellipses. To do so, you can use either of the Lasso tools.

To use the Lasso tools:

1. Press the Lasso tool in the Toolbox and choose either the regular or the polygon lasso ⬤.

2. In the regular lasso mode, drag around the area you want to select. The marching ants indicate the selected area ⬤.

3. In the polygon lasso mode, click the cursor around the area you want to select. Each click creates the point of a polygon ⬤.

4. Use the edge list in the Tool Options panel to choose among Hard Edge, Anti-Alias, or Feather (*see previous page*).

TIP The regular lasso is useful for following the curved contours of images. The polygon lasso is best for creating straight line shapes.

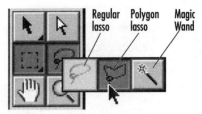

⬤ The **Lasso tools** *in the Toolbox*

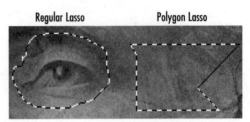

⬤ *A comparison of the Regular Lasso and the Polygon Lasso*

❽ *The **Magic Wand** in the Toolbox*

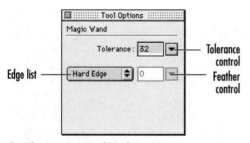

Edge list — Tolerance control — Feather control

❾ *The Magic Wand Tool Options*

You can also select areas by their color. For instance, you might want to select the background behind an image and then delete it or change its color. To do this, you use the Magic Wand.

To use the Magic Wand:

1. Press the Lasso tool to choose the Magic Wand in the Toolbox ❽.

2. In the Magic Wand Tool Options panel ❾, use the Tolerance slider or type a number in the field.

3. Use the edge list in the Tool Options panel to choose among Hard Edge, Anti-Alias, or Feather (*see page 133*).

4. Click the area you want to select. The marching ants indicate the selected area ❿.

TIP Tolerance controls how many colors the Magic Wand selects adjacent to the pixel you click. The lowest tolerance, 0, selects only one color, the exact color of the pixel you select with the tip of the Magic Wand. Increasing the tolerance up to the highest setting, 255, selects a greater range of colors.

❿ *The area selected with the Magic Wand*

Magic Wand

You may find that the Magic Wand tool has selected too little area, or you may find you need a different shape. You can change a selected area by using modifier keys with the selection tools.

To change the shape of selections:

With an area selected, use any of the selection tools.

- Hold the Shift key to add to the selected area. A plus (+) sign indicates you are adding to the selection ⓫.

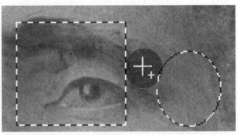

⓫ *Hold the Shift key to* add to a selection

- Hold the Option/Alt key to delete from the selected area. A minus (–) sign indicates you are subtracting from the selection ⓬.

TIP You can switch tools at any time. For instance, if the original selection was created by the Magic Wand, you can use the Lasso to modify it.

TIP The additional selection does not have to touch the original. For instance, you can select the top and bottom of an image, leaving the middle untouched.

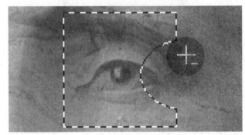

⓬ *Hold the Option/Alt key to* delete from a selection

Rather than use selections tools, you can also use the Fireworks selection commands for images.

To use the Selection commands:

- Choose **Select > All** to select all the pixels in the image.

- Choose **Select > None** to deselect the pixels enclosed by the marching ants.

  or

  Click one of the selection tools outside the selected area to deselect the pixels.

- Choose **Select > Inverse** to swap the status of the selected pixels, that is, deselect the selected pixels and select everything else.

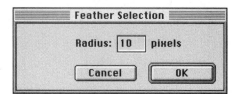

⑬ *The* Move Guide *dialog box*

Once you have selected a certain area with the Magic Wand, you might not want to keep clicking to select similar colors.

To use the Similar command:

With an area selected, choose **Select** > **Similar**. This selects all the areas of the entire image that have the same color.

TIP The Similar command uses the tolerance set for the Magic Wand.

TIP You can also use the Similar command on selections created by the Marquee or Lasso tools.

Sometimes it may be easier to select an area with the feather option turned off and then feather the edge afterwards.

To feather an existing selection:

1. With the area selected, choose **Select** > **Feather** to open the Feather Selection dialog box **⑬**.

2. Enter the number of pixels that you want to blur along the edge of the selection and then click OK.

TIP The marching ants may not change their appearance when you feather a selection. You can see the feathering when you move or color the selection.

Select Similar; Feather Selections

Fireworks also gives you a full set of drawing tools to use on images. Most of the tools work almost the same way as they do in the object mode. However, there are some important differences. The Rubber Stamp tool, for example, is available for use only on pixel images, not vector objects. This tool lets you copy and paint an image from one area onto another.

⓮ *The* **Rubber Stamp** *in the Toolbox*

To set the Rubber Stamp options:

1. Choose the Rubber Stamp tool in the Toolbox ⓮.

2. In the Rubber Stamp Tool Options ⓯, use the source list to choose Aligned Source or Fixed Source.

   TIP Use Aligned Source when you want to be able to release the mouse button but not lose the position of the area you are copying. This is useful when working on large images.

   TIP Use Fixed Source when you want to make multiple copies of one image. Each time you release the mouse, the source is restored to the original position.

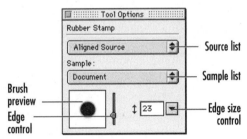

⓯ *The* **Rubber Stamp** *in the Toolbox*

3. Use the Sample list to choose Image or Document.

   TIP Image allows the Rubber Stamp to sample only the area inside the image. Document allows the Rubber Stamp to sample anywhere inside the document. This means you can sample the look of vector objects to paint them as pixels.

4. Use the edge size control to specify the size of the Rubber Stamp brush.

5. Use the edge softness control to change the softness of the Rubber Stamp edge.

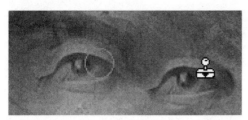

⑯ *Painting with the Rubber Stamp*

To use the Rubber Stamp tool:

1. Position the Rubber Stamp tool over the image and click to define the source: the area that you want to copy. A circle indicates the source area.

2. Move the Rubber Stamp tool to the area where you want to copy the source.

3. Drag with the Rubber Stamp. The source circle follows your movements indicating the area being copied from. The Rubber Stamp acts like a brush that paints with the image that appears under the source ⑯.

4. To change the source, hold the Option/Alt key and click on a new area. Then paint with the Rubber Stamp tool with the new source area.

TIP The Rubber Stamp tool does not act like a real rubber stamp. Digital rubber stamps (such as the ones found in Fireworks or Photoshop) simply copy the image from one area and paint it onto another. They do not recognize specific shapes or items. If you drag with the Rubber Stamp in a large enough area, you copy the image from one area to another.

Rubber Stamp

The Eraser works very differently from its vector counterpart. Rather than cutting paths, the Eraser in the image edit mode paints with a color or deletes pixels from an area.

To set the Eraser options:

1. Choose the Eraser in the Toolbox ⓲.

2. In the Eraser Tool Options ⓲, choose between the round or square shape.

3. Use the edge size control to open the slider or use the field to type the size of the Eraser.

4. Use the softness control to change the softness of the Eraser edge.

5. Use the Erase-to list to choose Transparent, Fill Color, Brush Color, or Canvas Color.

TIP The Erase-to-Transparent option is only available on image objects on layers. If you use the Eraser set to transparent on the background layer, you actually erase by painting with the canvas color.

TIP The Erase-to-Transparent option allows you to create images with irregular edges. This creates a very interesting look in combination with a shadow or bevel ⓳.

⓲ *The* **Eraser** *in the Toolbox*

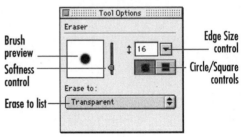

Brush preview — Softness control — Erase to list — Edge Size control — Circle/Square controls

⓲ *The* **Eraser Tool Options**

⓳ *The effects of* **erasing to transparent** *and then applying effects to the image*

**㉚** *The* Eyedropper *in the Toolbox*

The Eyedropper allows you to choose colors by sampling them from images.

To use the Eyedropper:

1. Choose the Eyedropper tool in the Toolbox **㉚**.

2. Click the Eyedropper in the image where you want to pick up a color. The color is applied to either the fill or stroke color, depending on which is currently selected in the Toolbox.

㉑ *The* Paint Bucket *in the Toolbox*

When you work with vector objects, you can use the Paint Bucket to change the appearance of gradients and patterns (*see page 86*). With image objects, the Paint Bucket acts as a speedy way to fill an area with a color.

To use the Paint Bucket:

1. Choose the Paint Bucket tool in the Toolbox **㉑**.

2. Click the Paint Bucket over the image. This fills the image with the currently selected Fill color.

TIP If the image has a selection around an area and you click the Paint Bucket within the selected area, the Paint Bucket fills only within the selected portion of the image.

TIP The rest of the drawing tools behave much the way they do when you create vector objects. The main difference is that they paint colors directly on the image, rather than creating paths.

Eyedropper; Paint Bucket

XTRAS 13

Xtras are features that are added to Fireworks. There are nine Xtras included as part of Fireworks. (If they are included as part of Fireworks, are they really extras?) These nine Xtras change the appearance of pixel images in Fireworks in different ways. You can also use the plug-ins for programs such as Adobe Photoshop within Fireworks.

In this chapter you will learn how to

Apply Xtras to vector objects.

Blur images.

Apply the Gaussian blur

Sharpen images.

Aply the Unsharp Mask.

Invert images.

Find Edges.

Mask using the Convert to Alpha Xtra.

Reapply Xtras quickly.

Add Xtras from other companies.

Change the image area to make Xtras work better.

Xtras work only on pixel objects. However, you can apply Xtras to vector objects as long as you recognize that you are converting the vector object to a pixel image.

To apply Xtras to vector objects:

1. Select one or more vector objects.

2. Choose an Xtra from the Xtras menu. A dialog box appears indicating that the image will be converted into a pixel image ❶.

3. Click OK. The object is converted and the Xtra is applied.

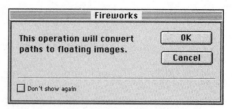

❶ *The dialog box that appears when you want to* apply an Xtra to a vector object

Three Xtras create different types of blur effects. The first two, Blur and Blur More, are applied via a simple menu command. These two blur commands are useful for concealing small imperfections in a scan. They can also help erase the lines between images that have been composited together.

To apply the Blur and Blur More Xtras:

1. Select an object or image.

2. Choose Xtras > Blur > Blur to give the image a slight blur effect ❷.

   or

2. Choose Xtras > Blur > Blur More to give the image a greater blur effect ❸.

TIP The blur Xtras work by changing some of the blacks and whites in an image to shades of gray. This means that some of the detail of an image is lost.

❷ *The effect of applying the* **Blur Xtra** *to an image*

❸ *The effect of applying the* **Blur More Xtra** *to an image*

Preview
area

Zoom | Zoom | Radius
in | out | slider

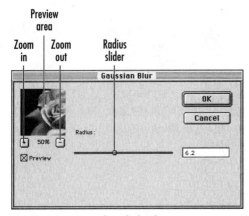

❹ *The* **Gaussian Blur** *dialog box*

Original   Gaussian Blur

❺ *The effect of applying the* **Gaussian Blur Xtra** *to an image*

The third blur effect, Gaussian Blur, is applied through a dialog box. The Gaussian Blur Xtra gives you more control over the amount of the blur. This blur is useful for making objects appear as if they are positioned behind others.

To apply the Gaussian Blur Xtra:

1. Select an object or image.

2. Choose **Xtras** > **Blur** > **Gaussian Blur**. The Gaussian Blur dialog box appears ❹.

3. Use the slider to increase or decrease the amount of the blur.

4. Use the Preview area to see the effects of the blur.

5. Press and drag inside the Preview area to see a different portion of the image.

6. Click the plus sign (+) to zoom in on the Preview area.

7. Click the minus sign (–) to zoom out from the Preview area.

8. When you are satisfied with the look of the Gaussian Blur, click OK to apply the Xtra ❺.

Gaussian Blur

Just as you can blur images, so can you sharpen them. This is especially useful when working with scanned images that tend to look a little soft, or out of focus. Three different sharpen Xtras come with Fireworks. The first two Xtras sharpen the image very simply, with little control over how the sharpening is added.

To apply the Sharpen and Sharpen More Xtras:

1. Select an object or image.

2. Choose **Xtras > Sharpen > Sharpen** to slightly sharpen the image ❻.

    or

    Choose **Xtras > Sharpen > Sharpen More** to sharpen the image slightly more ❼.

TIP The sharpen Xtras work by changing some gray pixels in the image to black or white. Although it may seen that more detail is revealed, strictly speaking some of the detail is lost.

❻ *The effect of applying the* Sharpen Xtra *to an image*

❼ *The effect of applying the* **Sharpen More Xtra** *to an image*

Preview Threshold Radius
area   slider   slider

Zoom   Zoom   Amount
in   out   slider

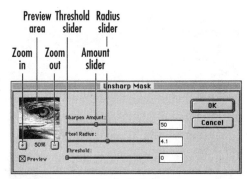

❽ *The* Unsharp Mask *dialog box*

Original   Unsharp Mask Xtra

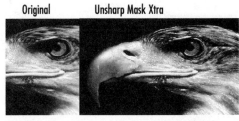

❾ *The effect of applying the* **Unsharp Mask Xtra** *to an image*

Original   Unsharp Mask Xtra at high settings

❿ *Using the Unsharp Mask Xtra at high settings can create a glow around objects.*

The third sharpen Xtra is the Unsharp Mask Xtra. Despite its name, this filter does sharpen images, and does so in a very sophisticated fashion. This is the most widely used command to compensate for the blurring that occurs when scanning images.

To apply the Unsharp Mask Xtra:

1. Select an object or image.

2. Choose **Xtras > Sharpen > Unsharp Mask**. The Unsharp Mask dialog box appears **❽**.

3. Drag the Amount slider or type in the field to change the amount of contrast that is applied—the greater the amount, the greater the sharpening.

4. Drag the Threshold slider or type in the field to set how different the pixels must be before they are sharpened.

TIP A Threshold of 0 means that all the pixels in the image are sharpened.

TIP A low threshold means that pixels that are only slightly different in brightness are sharpened. A high threshold means that only those pixels that are very different in brightness are sharpened. For instance, in illustration **❾**, a high threshold means that only the sharp line in the beak would be sharpened. A low threshold means that the gray feathers in the lower-right corner would be sharpened.

5. Drag the Radius slider or type in the field to set the number of pixels around the edge that have the sharpening effect applied.

6. Click OK to see the effects of the Unsharp Mask Xtra **❾**.

TIP High Unsharp Mask settings with a low threshold can cause an unwanted glow around objects **❿**.

The Invert Xtra reverses selected images into negatives. Black becomes white; red becomes green; yellow becomes blue; and so on.

To apply the Invert Xtra:

1. Select an object or image.

2. Choose **Xtras** > **Invert** > **Invert**. The colors of the image are reversed **⑪**.

Original   Invert Xtra

⑪ *The effect of applying the* **Invert Xtra** *to an image*

The Find Edges Xtra looks for pixels in the image with different shades or colors. Boundaries between the colors are considered edges. The Find Edges Xtra changes the colors of the pixels so that a line appears where there was an edge. This gives the effect of converting photographs into line art.

To apply the Find Edges Xtra:

1. Select an object or image.

2. Choose **Xtras** > **Other** > **Find Edges**. The image is converted **⑫**.

TIP Photographs tend to appear white on black after applying the Find Edges Xtra. Use the Invert Xtra after the Find Edges command to convert the image to black on white.

Original   Find Edges Xtra

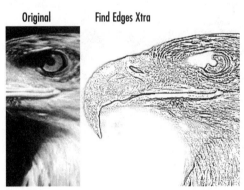

⑫ *The effect of applying the* **Find Edges Xtra** *and then the Invert Xtra to an image*

⓭ *To* **create an Alpha mask** *draw a rectangle over an image and then apply a gradient.*

⓮ *The result of* applying the Convert to Alpha Xtra *to a gradient*

⓯ *The result of applying* the Mask Group

The next Xtra, Convert to Alpha, lets you create very sophisticated masking techniques. While the procedure to apply the Xtra is very simple, pay careful attention to how the results can be used.

To mask using the Convert to Alpha Xtra:

1. Find an object or image to mask. For instance, you might want a scanned image to fade in intensity from top to bottom.

2. Draw a rectangle that covers the image you want to fade and position it over the original object or image **⓭**.

3. Fill the rectangle with a gradient that changes from black at the top to white at the bottom.

TIP When working with Alpha masks, remember that Alpha areas that are black allow the images underneath to be seen. Alpha areas that are white make the images underneath transparent. Alpha values between black and white show the images with amounts of transparency in between.

4. With the rectangle selected, choose **Xtras > Other > Convert to Alpha**. This converts the vector object to a grayscale image that can be used as an Alpha mask **⓮**.

5. Select both the original image and the Alpha mask and choose **Modify > Mask Group**. The original image is seen through the Alpha mask **⓯**.

TIP The Alpha masks in Fireworks are similar to the Alpha channels in Adobe Photoshop. However, the Fireworks Alpha masks can be applied on an object-by-object basis, rather than an entire layer as in Photoshop.

Convert to Alpha

Once you have applied an Xtra, it appears as the Repeat [Xtra] command.

To reapply Xtras quickly:

With an object selected, choose **Xtras** > **Repeat [Name of Xtra]**. The Repeat [Xtra] command also has a keystroke to make it even easier to reapply an Xtra.

TIP The Mac keystroke for the Repeat [Xtra] command is Command-Option-Shift-X.

TIP The Win keystroke for the Repeat [Xtra] command is Ctrl-Alt-Shift-X.

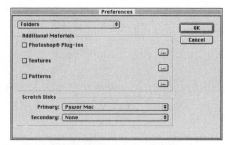

16 *The* **Mac Folders Preferences** *dialog box*

In addition to the Xtras that come with Fireworks, you can also use any Photoshop-compatible plug-ins. These plug-ins can be installed into their own folder for Fireworks, or they can be the ones currently used by Photoshop or other applications.

To add Xtras from other companies:

1. Choose **File** > **Preferences**. This open the Preferences dialog box.

2. On the Mac press the pop-up list to choose Folders. This open the settings for choosing other folders for Fireworks features **16**.

   or

   On Windows click the Folders tab **17**.

3. Click the box next to Photoshop Plug-ins and then click the ellipsis button.

4. Navigate to find plug-ins folder and then click the select button.

TIP The Xtras do not appear in the Fireworks Xtras menu until after you restart Fireworks.

TIP Once you have added Xtras from other companies they can be applied just as the built-in Fireworks Xtras.

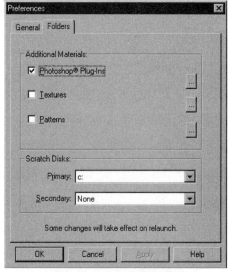

17 *The* **Windows Additional Materials Preferences** *dialog box*

Repeat [Xtra] Command; Add Xtras

⑱ *Xtras such as the Gaussian Blur cannot work on the edges of objects without space added to the image.*

If you are working with Xtras, you may find that you need more space around the image so that the Xtra gives you the proper effect **⑱**. For instance, the Gaussian Blur does not blur the edges of an image. Fortunately, you can work around that by increasing the area around an image.

To increase the area around an image:

1. Draw a rectangle larger than the image.

2. Fill the rectangle with the canvas color.

3. Choose **Modify > Arrange > Send to Back**.

4. Select both the rectangle and the image and choose **Select > Convert to Image**. This adds area around the image which makes it easier to create certain effects with Xtras **⑲**.

⑲ **Adding extra space around the image** *allows the Xtra to work on the outside of the image.*

Although Fireworks boasts a wealth of tools, fills, and effects, it cannot do everything. So it is very likely that you have artwork created in other programs that you want to import into Fireworks. For instance, you probably have scans saved in pixel programs such as Adobe Photoshop. You might also have logos and other artwork created in vector programs such as FreeHand or Illustrator. There are many different considerations for importing artwork into Fireworks. The factors depend on the software that created the original artwork as well as the type of Web graphic you want to create.

In this chapter you will learn how to

Open scans as a background layer.

Import scans as image objects.

Open Photoshop layered artwork.

Import Photoshop layered artwork.

Open vector artwork.

Set the size of vector artwork.

Set the pages of vector artwork.

Set the layers of vector artwork.

Render vector art into pixel images.

Set the edge of vector artwork.

Set additional folders for textures or patterns.

macromedia
FIREWORKS

You can bring scans into Fireworks two different ways. The first is to open a scan, making it the background layer.

To open a scan as a background layer:

1. Choose **File>Open** and then choose the scan you want to open.

2. Click OK. The scan automatically opens as the background layer of the Fireworks document ❶.

TIP The Fireworks document opens with the same resolution and size as the original scan.

❶ *A scan* **opened as the Background layer** *of a Fireworks document*

You can also import scans into Fireworks.

To import scans as image objects:

1. Choose **File>Import** and then find the scan you want to import. Click OK. A small corner symbol indicates the file is ready for placing on the currently selected Fireworks layer.

2. Drag the corner symbol to draw a rectangle that the scan will scale to fit.

   or

   Click to place the scanned image at the original size.

3. The scan appears as an image object on the currently selected object layer ❷. (*For more information on working with image objects, see Chapter 11, "Pixel Images."*)

TIP Use the Drop Selection command (*see page 129*) to place imported image objects onto the background layer.

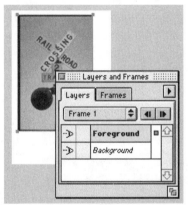

❷ *A scan* **imported as an image object on a layer** *of a Fireworks document*

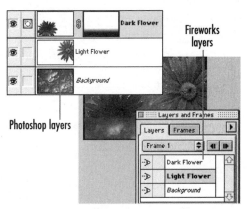

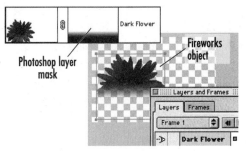

❸ Photoshop documents open in Fireworks *with their layers intact.*

❹ *How a Photoshop* layer mask opens in Fireworks

Fireworks can also open native Photoshop files without losing the separate layers.

To open Photoshop layered artwork:

1. Choose **File**>**Open** and then find the Photoshop file you want to open.

2. Click OK. The file opens as a Fireworks document with the same layers as in the original Photoshop file **❸**.

TIP Photoshop layer masks are applied to the image with transparent areas outside the mask **❹**.

When you open Photoshop files in Fireworks, they open with their layers intact. However, there is a difference when you import Photoshop files.

To import Photoshop layered artwork:

1. Choose **File**>**Import** and then find the Photoshop layered artwork that you want to import. Click OK.

2. Click or drag to place the artwork.

3. The artwork appears as different types of image objects on the currently selected object layer **❺**.

TIP Choose **File**>**Preferences** to control how Photoshop files are imported, either with layers or flattened.

TIP Use the import command if you need to add Photoshop elements to an existing Fireworks document. Use the open command if you want to maintain Photoshop layers.

TIP Photoshop layer masks are applied to the image with transparent areas outside the mask.

❺ *How Photoshop layers are* **imported as image objects** *into Fireworks*

Fireworks can also open artwork created in vector-drawing programs such as Macromedia FreeHand, Adobe Illustrator or CorelDraw. Those objects open in Fireworks as vector objects. This means you can use the more sophisticated tools in the vector-drawing programs and then add those objects to your Fireworks document as editable objects.

To open vector artwork:

1. Choose **File**>**Open** and then find the vector file you want to open. Click OK. The Vector File Options dialog box appears **⊘**.

2. Set the options for opening the vector artwork. (*See the instructions that follow here and on pages 157–158 for specific details.*)

To set the size of imported vector artwork:

1. Open the artwork in Fireworks and use the top third of the Vector File Options dialog box.

2. Use the Scale control to import the art at a specific size compared to its original size.

   or

   Change the width or height field to change the size of the art to fit a space.

   or

   Set the resolution to something other than 72 pixels per inch to change the size of the art.

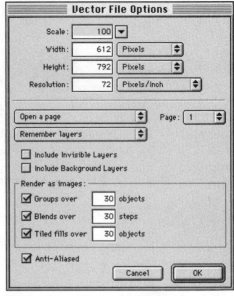

⊘ *The* Vector File Options *dialog box*

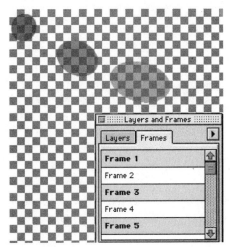

❼ *A composite of how a* vector blend imports into Fireworks onto individual frames

If your artwork has pages or layers, you can set how those pages or layers are opened.

To set which pages of vector artwork to open:

1. Choose **File** > **Open** and then find the vector file you want to open. Click OK. The Vector File Options dialog box appears.

2. Use the page number list to choose which page is imported.

   or

   Choose Open Pages As Frames from the Open As list to open each of the pages as a Fireworks frame.

TIP Opening multiple pages as frame makes it easy to convert vector artwork into animations.

To set the layers of opened vector artwork:

1. With the vector artwork open in Fireworks, in the Vector File Options dialog box choose Remember layers to import the layers as Fireworks layers.

   or

   Choose Ignore layers to import the artwork onto one Fireworks layer.

   or

   Choose Convert layers to frames to open each of the layers as a Fireworks frame.

TIP If you use FreeHand, you can set its blends to appear on individual layers. Opening that document with Convert layers to frames in Fireworks allows you to animate the blend **❼**.

2. Check Include Invisible Layers to bring in artwork on the layers that are not visible in the vector program, if necessary.

3. Check Include Background Layers to bring in artwork on the background layers in FreeHand, if necessary.

Because vector artwork can easily contain hundreds of objects, you may not want all those objects opened as individual vector objects. Fireworks lets you convert some of the vector objects into pixel images.

To render imported vector art into pixel images:

1. In the Vector File Options dialog box check Groups Over and fill in the field to set what type of groups should be converted into pixel images.

2. Check Blends over and fill in the field to set what types of blends should be converted into pixel images.

3. Check Tiled fills and fill in the field to set what types of tiled fills, or patterns, should be converted into pixel images.

TIP Rendering vectors as pixels helps when importing photorealistic or very intricate images ➑.

When you open vector artwork in Fireworks, you have a choice as to how the artwork appears: either with a hard edge or a softer, anti-aliased edge.

To set the edge of opened vector artwork:

In the Vector File Options dialog box, check Anti-Aliased to import the artwork with the Fill edge setting as Anti-Aliased.

or

Deselect Anti-Aliased to import the artwork with the Fill edge setting as Hard Edge (*see page 83*).

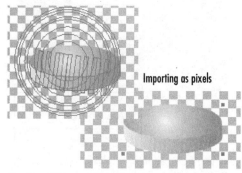

Importing as vectors

Importing as pixels

➑ *The difference between importing as vectors and rendering the vector objects as pixel images.*

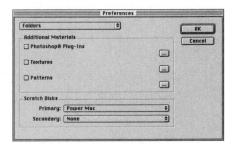

⑨ *The Mac* **Preferences** *dialog box*

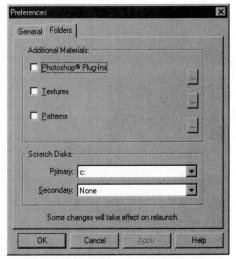

⑩ *The Windows* **Preferences** *dialog box*

Importing does not just mean bringing in artwork. Fireworks also lets you set a specific folder that holds the artwork that is used for textures or patterns

To set additional folders for textures or patterns:

1. Choose **File > Preferences**. This opens the Preferences dialog box.

2. On the Mac use the pop-up list to choose Folders. This open the settings for choosing other folders for Fireworks features **⑨**.

   or

   On Windows click the Folders tab **⑩**.

3. Click the box next to Textures, click the ellipsis button, and then navigate to find the folder that holds the textures.

4. Do the same to set the folder for the patterns.

TIP Textures and patterns can be saved as PNG format.

TIP The textures and patterns do not appear in the pop-up lists until after you restart Fireworks.

Set Folders for Textures and Patterns

BASIC EXPORTING 15

Converting graphics and exporting them embody the very heart and soul of the Fireworks application. In fact, you may have started learning about Fireworks by skipping directly to this chapter. Even if you never use the drawing tools, Fireworks gives you exceptionally simple yet powerful ways to convert images one at a time or in batches for the Web or for other graphics programs. This chapter covers the basics of converting and exporting; Chapter 18 covers settings for exporting rollovers and Chapter 19 covers exporting animations.

In this chapter you will learn how to

Convert and export images.

Open and work within the Export Preview window.

Decide between GIF or JPEG.

Set the GIF palette options.

Save and load palettes.

Set the JPEG options.

Create images that appear gradually.

Compare export settings.

Create a Transparent GIF.

Save export settings.

Export in other file formats.

Batch process images.

Scale an exported image.

Export a portion of an image.

Use the Export Wizard.

This first exercise gives a real quick start in exporting using Fireworks to anyone who already knows enough about Web graphics to be able to choose the export settings without assistance. If you are new to Web graphics, the exercises through the rest of this chapter give details on which settings are right for different situations.

To export an image:

1. With a file open choose **File> Export** to open the Export Preview ❶ and adjust the image in the preview area or zoom in or out, if necessary. (*See page 163.*)

2. Choose a file format. (*See pages 164 or pages 172 for more about files formats.*)

3. Choose a color palette and how many colors should be used in the palette. (*See pages 165–167 for details on color palette and number of colors.*)

4. Make the image background transparent, if necessary. (*See the techniques on page 171.*)

5. Choose compression settings, if necessary, to make the image smaller. (*See page 169 for more details.*)

6. Compare the look, file size, and loading speed of the different settings you are considering to determine which one is best. (*See page 170 for details on making those comparisons.*)

7. If desired, set the graphic to load as interlaced or progressive. (*See page 169 for explanations of those settings.*)

8. If you expect to export other images the same way, save the export settings to use again. (*See page 172 in this chapter.*)

9. Click Export and use the dialog box to give the file a name and save it in the proper location.

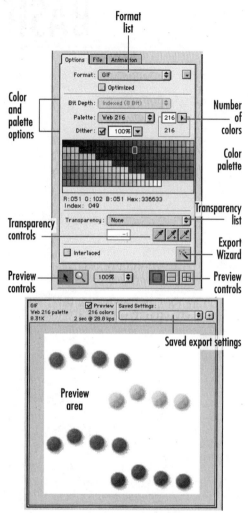

❶ *The two sides of the* **Export Preview** *window*

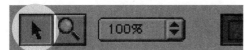

❷ *The* **Pointer Tool** *in the Export Preview window*

In order to set any of the export or conversion features, you must first open the Export Preview window.

To open the Export Preview window:

Choose **File** > **Export** to open the Export Preview window **❶**.

❸ *The* **Hand cursor** *lets you move the image within the Preview area.*

As soon as you open the Export Preview window, you see a preview of the image in the file. There are several different ways to control the magnification and area shown within the Preview area.

To change the Preview area views:

1. To move the image within the Preview area, select the Pointer tool **❷** and drag the image. The Hand cursor moves the image within the Preview area **❸**.

2. Use the magnification list **❹** to choose one of the preset magnifications.

   or

   To zoom in on a specific area of the image, select the Zoom In/Out tool and click the image **❺**.

   TIP Hold the Option/Alt key to zoom out from the image.

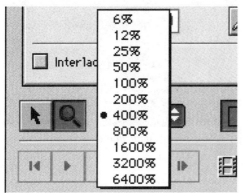

❹ *The* **Magnification list** *in the Export Preview window*

❺ *The* **Zoom tool** *lets you zoom in or out of the Preview area.*

The first choice you need to make in exporting a graphic is which format you need. For basic exporting to the Web, choose either GIF or JPEG. (*Fireworks does export in formats for uses besides the Web; for a brief explanation of those formats see page 163.*)

GIF or JPEG?

As a general rule, use the GIF format for images with flat or solid areas of color ❻. Plain type, solid fills, cartoons, and flat-color logos usually look best when saved as GIF images. GIF images are 8-bit files, which mean they are limited to 256 colors.

❻ *The type of image that converts well as a GIF*

Use the JPEG format for photographic images or images with subtle blends ❼. JPEG images are 24-bit images with up to 16.7 millions of colors. When people with 8-bit monitors view a JPEG image, they do not see millions of colors. Only those with high-quality monitors will see all the colors in your image. (*For a color comparison of GIF and JPEG images, see the color insert.*)

TIP If an image has both flat art and a photograph, dithering a GIF image may help maintain the photograph as well as the flat art.

TIP Slicing images can also help work with images that combine photos and flat art (*see page 189*).

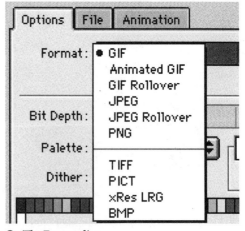

❼ *The type of graphic that converts well as a JPEG image*

To choose a file format:

Use the Format list ❽ to choose a fromat. For Web graphics choose GIF or JPEG. These are the two main formats for exporting static images on the Web.

(*For exporting in the the GIF Rollover or JPEG Rollover formats, see Chapter 18, "Rollovers." For exporting in the Animated GIF format, see Chapter 19, "Animations."*)

❽ *The* **Format** *list*

GIF or JPEG; File Format

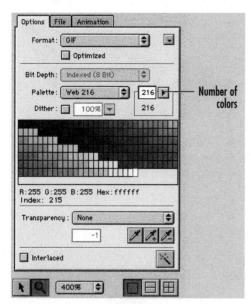

Number of colors

❾ *The* **GIF format** *options*

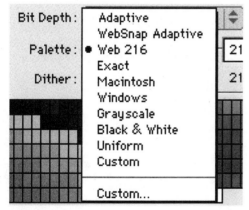

❿ *The* **Palette** *list*

When working with a GIF file, you have many other choices for exporting the file. The primary choice is the type of color palette used to create the image. The three choices for GIF graphics are Web 216, Adaptive, and WebSnap Adaptive. Web 216 palette lets you limit your GIF image to only Web-safe colors. These are the 216 colors that will always look the same no matter what browser or platform people use to view your site.

To set the GIF Web 216 palette options:

1. Choose GIF from the Export Preview window Format list. This gives you the GIF options **❾**.

2. Choose Web 216 from the Palette list **❿**.

TIP This limits the colors in the file to the Web-safe colors. However, most GIF images do not need 216 colors to display properly.

3. Use the Maximum number of colors list to reduce the number of colors in the document.

TIP As you reduce the number of colors, Fireworks automatically changes the the artwork in the Preview area.

4. If necessary, check the Dither option to create a mixture between two colors to create the look of a third.

TIP It is rarely necessary to dither in Fireworks; dither only if all other options are unsatisfactory.

5. If you choose the Dither option, use the slider to change the dither amount.

6. Check Optimized to automatically lower the number of colors in the document to the minimum amount.

You do not have to limit yourself to just the 216 Web-safe colors ⑪. You can choose an *Adaptive* palette. Adaptive means that Fireworks first chooses those colors in the image that match the Web-safe palette. It then adds the non–Web-safe colors ⑫. This means that you have a combination of colors that are Web-safe and not Web-safe. (*For a comparison of the results converting images using Web 216 or Adaptive palettes, see the color insert.*)

To set the GIF Adaptive palette options:

1. Choose GIF from the Export Preview window Format list.

2. Choose Adaptive from the Palette list.

3. Use the rest of the GIF palette options described in the previous exercise to lower the number of colors in the document.

TIP If you choose an Adaptive palette means that when your artwork is viewed on an 8-bit monitor, the colors will be dithered.

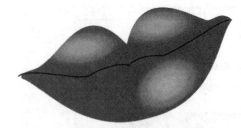

⑪ *The* **Web-safe palette** *limits shades and blends to the Web-safe colors. This can cause unwanted dithering and banding.*

⑫ *The* **Adaptive palette** *allows a mixture of Web-safe and other colors. This gives smoother looks for blends, shades, and shadows.*

Other palette options

- Use Macintosh or Windows palettes when creating artwork for presentations or software to be shown on a specific platform.

- Choose Grayscale or Black and White for certain print applications.

- Choose Custom to open a swatches palette saved from Fireworks or from Photoshop.

⓭ *The type of image that converts well using the* **WebSnap Adaptive palette.** *This allows the flat color areas to stay within Web-safe colors while the photograph uses an adaptive palette of many other colors.*

The final GIF palette is the WebSnap Adaptive palette. When this palette is chosen, Fireworks looks at all the colors in the image. The Web-safe colors are added first. Then all the other colors are added. However, if a color is within 7 units of a Web-safe color, that color is converted into a Web-safe color.

The benefit of working with the WebSnap Adaptive palette is that areas filled with flat color do not get dithered when viewed on monitors that can only show 256 colors. (*For a color illustration of how the WebSnap Adaptive palette works, see the color insert.*)

To set the WebSnap Adaptive palette options:

1. Choose GIF from the Export Preview window Format list.

2. Choose WebSnap Adaptive from the Palette list.

3. Use the rest of the GIF palette options described in the exercise on page 165 to lower the number of colors in the document.

TIP The WebSnap Adaptive palette is excellent for images that combine both flat colors and photographic images ⓭.

GIF WebSnap Adaptive Paltte

Once you have created an Adaptive palette, you can then save that palette to use in othe images. This can help give your site a unified appearance without needing to dither images.

To save a palette:

1. Choose Save Palette from the Palette pop-up list **⑭** in the Export Preview window.

2. Name the palette and specify where you want to save it. ·

3. Click Save to save the palette.

TIP Use Macintosh or Windows palettes when creating artwork for presentations or software to be shown on a specific platform.

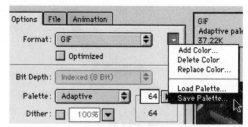

⑭ *Choose* **Save Palette** *to save a specific palette to use when exporting other images.*

You can also load palettes to use when exporting images.

To load a palette:

1. Choose Load Palette from the Palette pop-up list in the Export Preview window.

2. Find the palette you want to load and then click OK.

TIP Fireworks can load palettes saved using Adobe Photoshop.

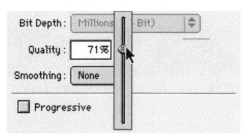

⓭ *The* **JPEG Quality** *slider*

No Smoothing   Smoothing at setting 2

⓰ **Adding Smoothing** *to a JPEG can reduce the coarseness of the image, but it blurs the image.*

⓱ *How* **interlaced or progressive images** *appear as they are downloaded into a file*

As discussed earlier in this chapter, the JPEG file format allows you to keep more colors in your document. The size of the file is lowered by *compressing* the image. Unlike some compressions that save all the information in an image, JPEG compressions are *lossy*. This means that information in the image is thrown away, or lost, as the image is made smaller. (*For a color illustration of saving with various compression settings, see the color insert.*)

To set the JPEG options:

1. Choose JPEG from the Format list.

2. Drag the quality slider to change the file size—the lower the quality, the smaller the file **⓭**.

TIP Lowering the file size can make the image look coarse or splotchy.

3. Set the Smoothing amount to slightly blur the image. This softens the effects of lowering the file quality **⓰**. (*See the color insert for examples of the various JPEG settings.*)

TIP Do not use JPEG compression on your only copy of a file because you lose information in the image. Save the file as a Fireworks PNG file to preserve all the information.

You have a choice as to how your graphics are revealed as they are downloaded. You can set the image to be revealed gradually **⓱**. This lets visitors decide faster whether or not the image is important to see completely.

To create images that appear gradually:

For GIF images choose Interlaced.

or

For JPEG images choose Progressive.

JPEG Options; Images that Appear Gradually

Creating Web graphics is a balancing act between lowering the file size and maintaining the image quality. With all the choices available, you might find it hard to remember which setting gave you the best image. Fireworks lets you compare different settings so you can see for yourself which setting produces the best image while lowering the file size. This is one of the most important aspects of working within the Export Preview window.

To compare export settings:

1. In the Export Preview window, change from the 1-Preview icon to either the 2- or 4-Preview icons **⑱**. This divides the Preview area into smaller sections **⑲**.

2. Click each of the sections to set export options.

3. Compare the image quality as well as the file size and download time.

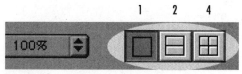

⑱ *The 1-, 2-, and 4-Preview Window* icons

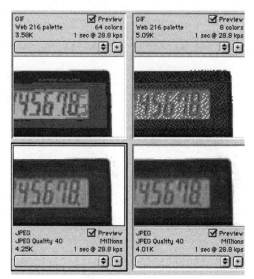

⑲ *The* **Preview area** *divided into four sections*

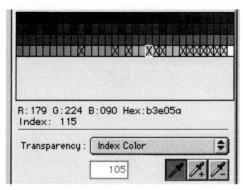

R:179 G:224 B:090 Hex:b3e05a
Index: 115

Transparency: Index Color

105

⓴ *The* **Transparent GIF** *controls*

㉑ *The* **Eyedropper** *allows you to select those colors in the image that should be transparent.*

One of the main advantages of the GIF format is that certain areas of an image can be made to be transparent. This allows you to have a Web graphic that blends into the background of the page. There are two ways to create a transparent GIF. The first method lets you pick the colors within the color table and set them to be transparent.

To create a Transparent GIF (method #1):

1. Set the image that you want to make transparent over the background color of the Web page. This makes it easier to have the transparency blend smoothly.

2. Choose Index Color from the Transparency list.

3. Use the eyedropper to click the color in the color table that you want to make transparent. Transparent colors are displayed with an *X* through their box **⓴**.

4. Use the eyedropper with the plus (+) sign to select additional colors that should be transparent.

5. Use the eyedropper with the minus (–) sign to deselect colors.

The second method lets you pick the colors directly in the image.

To create a Transparent GIF (method #2):

1. Place the image over the background color of the Web page.

2. Choose Index Color from the Transparency list.

3. Use the eyedropper to click on that portion of the image that should be transparent **㉑**.

4. Use the plus eyedropper to add more colors to the transparency.

5. Use the minus eyedropper to delete colors from the transparency.

Once you have a certain set of export settings, you can save them for use later.

To save export settings:

1. Choose File>**Export** and set the Export settings to the way you want.

2. Click the Save Current Settings button at the top of the Preview windows ㉒ to open the Preset Name dialog box.

3. Give the settings a name and then click OK. This adds the settings to the Saved Settings list.

To use saved export settings:

1. Choose File>**Export**.

2. Choose the previously saved export setting from the the Saved Settings list ㉓.

3. Export the file as usual.

㉒ *The* Save Current Settings *button*

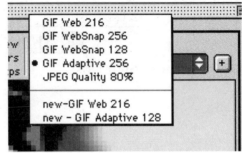

㉓ *The* Export preset *list*

Although Fireworks was designed for Web graphics, Fireworks does convert images for other purposes.

Exporting Other File Formats

Choose among the other file formats listed in the Export Preview window's format list.

- Choose **PNG** for on-screen presentations such as Microsoft PowerPoint, Macromedia Director or Authorware.

- Choose **PNG** for Web graphics that can be seen with specialized plug-ins.

- Choose **TIFF** for print graphics.

- Choose **PICT** (Mac) or **BMP** (Win) for applications such as Microsoft PowerPoint or Microsoft Word.

- Choose **xRes LRG** to convert your graphics to Macromedia's imaging program xRes.

Save Settings; Other File Formats

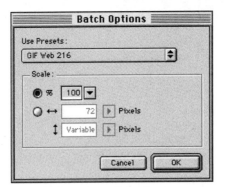

㉔ *The* Batch Options *dialog box*

You may need to convert many images at once into Web graphics. Fortunately, you do not have to manually open, choose the settings, export, and save each image one at a time. The Batch command automatically converts the contents of a directory (folder) using a saved export setting.

To batch-process images:

1. Place the images that all need the same kind of export settings in the same directory (folder).

2. Choose **File>Batch** and use the dialog box to navigate to the folder you want to convert.

3. Once you select the folder, the Batch Options dialog box appears **㉔**.

4. Choose an export preset from the Use Presets list.

5. If you want to change the size of the image, set the amount in the Scale percentage field.

   or

   Click the button to set the absolute size for the width and height.

6. Click OK to start the Batch processing.

Batch Process

While you cannot scale an entire Fireworks document, you can scale the document as part of the export process.

To scale an exported image:

1. Click the File tab of the Export Preview dialog box. This opens the File Scale and Export Area options **❷❺**.

2. Use the Percentage (%) slider or type in the field to scale the image to a percentage of its original size.

   or

   Enter an amount in the *W* (width) or *H* (height) fields to scale the image to an absolute measurement.

TIP With Constrain selected, the width and height of the image will always keep their proportions to the original image.

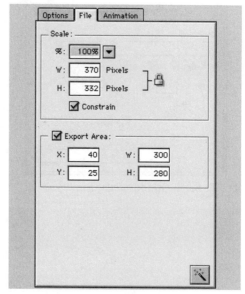

❷❺ *The* **File tab** *of the Export Preview dialog box shows the scale and export area options.*

As you are working on a document, you may want to export just a certain portion of the image. You can do this numerically within the Export Preview window.

To export a portion of an image numerically:

1. Select Export Area within the Export Area File tab.

2. Use the *X* and *Y* fields to set the upper left corner of the area to be exported.

3. Use the *W* and *H* fields to set the width and height of the exported area. A line appears around the area that will be exported **❷❻**.

4. Export the file as usual.

❷❻ *A* **dashed line** *indicates the exported area of an image.*

Scale an Exported Image; Export a Portion Numerically

㉗ *The* **Export Area** *tool in the Toolbox*

㉘ *Use the Export Area tool to* **drag a rectangle around the area you want to export.**

㉙ *Use the Export Area tool to* **drag a rectangle around the area you want to export.**

㉚ *Use* **Export Wizard dialog screens** *to select the proper export format for your image or analyze the current format.*

You can also export a portion of an image using the Export Area tool.

To use the Export Area tool:

1. Choose the Export Area tool from the Toolbox **㉗**.

2. Drag a rectangle around the area you want to export **㉘**.

3. Double-click inside the rectangle or click the Export button in the Tool Options panel. Only the selected area appears in the Export Preview window.

4. Export the file as usual.

If you are confused while exporting a file, you can use the Export Wizard to guide you through the settings.

To use the Export Wizard:

1. Choose **File** > **Export** and then click the Export Wizard icon in the Export Preview window **㉙**. This opens the Export Wizard screen **㉚**.

2. Click Select an export format to have the Export Wizard choose the format that is most appropriate for your image.

   or

   Click Analyze current settings to have Fireworks analyze whether or not the current format is appropriate.

3. Click Continue for each of the Export Wizard screens to complete the Export Wizard process.

IMAGE MAPS 16

One of the most important features of Web graphics is image mapping. This is the way to divide the areas of a graphic into links to other Web pages. So, for example, a graphic of the United States, could have links over the parts of the country. If viewers click over the area of the Northeast, it brings them to a Web page for that region. Similar links could be created over the Southeast, the Midwest, and so on. Fireworks makes it easy to assign links to areas of an image.

In this chapter you will learn how to

Open the URL toolbar.

Set the type of image map.

Create links for a document.

Edit existing links.

Duplicate links.

Delete links.

Delete unused links.

Draw URL objects.

Modify and move URL objects.

Apply links to URL objects.

Copy graphics to URL shapes.

Understand URL link choices.

macromedia
FIREWORKS

For the rest of these exercises it is important that you have the URL toolbar visible.

To open the URL toolbar:

If the URL toolbar is not visible, choose **Window** > **Toolbars** > **URLs** to open the URL toolbar ❶.

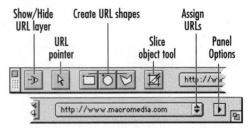

❶ *The* **URL** *toolbar* (*divided into two parts for space reasons*)

Two types of image maps exist, server-side and client-side. Client-side maps respond more quickly and can be run from any type of server; however, some very old browsers cannot read their information. Server-side maps require special scripts and the cooperation of your Internet service provider.

If the intended audience for your Web site includes people who might be using old browsers, consider server-side image maps. Given how popular the newer browsers have become, most Web sites, however, can easily use client-side image maps.

To set the type of image map:

1. Choose Image Map Options from the Panel Options list of the URL toolbar ❷.

2. In the Image Map Options dialog box ❸, use the Map Type list to choose Client-side, Server-side, or Both.

3. Use the Background URL list to set a URL link for the entire graphic. Other URL links can then be added over the background link.

4. Type in the Alternative Image Description field the text you would like to have shown if, for some reason, the browser does not display the image.

TIP Some people with slow Web connections set their browsers to not display images. Alternate Image Descriptions give them information about the image.

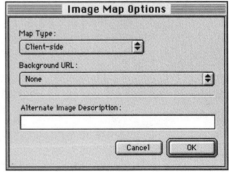

❷ *The* **Panel Options** *list*

❸ *The* **Image Map Options** *dialog box*

URL toolbar; Types of Image Maps

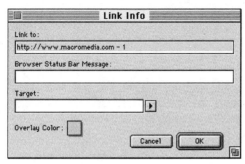

❹ *The **Link Info** dialog box*

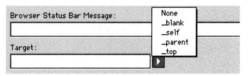

❺ *The **Move Guide** dialog box*

In order to assign URL links to the image map, you must create the links and add them the the URL toolbar.

To create links for a document:

1. Choose New Link from the Panel Options list of the URL toolbar to open the Link Info dialog box **❹**.

TIP Fireworks allows you to type in any type of URL link. The three most common URL links are http, mailto, and ftp. (*For an explanation of how to set these links, see page 183.*)

2. Type the URL information in the Link To field.

3. Type in the Browser Status Bar Message the information you would like shown in the browser to describe what the link is that users are passing over.

4. To target the link to open a new window or a specific frame, type the information in the Target field, or use one of the target presets **❺**.

5. Click the Overlay color box to open the Color Mixer. You can then set a new color for that link.

TIP Setting different colors for the various links makes it easy to see which areas of the graphic have which links applied to them.

Create Links

Web links are constantly changing. Rather than having to define new links for areas, you can edit existing links.

To edit existing links:

1. Choose a link in the URL toolbar.
2. Choose Edit Link **❻** from the Panel Options list to open the Link Info dialog box.
3. Make whatever changes you want to the link and then click OK. This updates all instances of the link in the graphic.

❻ *Choosing* **Edit Links** *from the Panel Options list*

If you have many links with similar URL addresses, it may be easier to duplicate the link and then edit its specific address.

To duplicate links:

1. Choose a link in the URL toolbar.
2. Choose Duplicate Link from the Panel Options list to open the Link Info dialog box.
3. Make whatever changes you want to the address information and then click OK.

You can also delete links from your files.

To delete links:

1. Choose a link in the URL toolbar.
2. Choose Delete Link from the Panel Options list. This deletes the link from the list as well as any URL objects (*see next page*) that have that URL as their Link To address.

You can also delete links that have not been applied to URL objects.

To delete unused links:

Choose Delete Unused Links from the Panel Options list in the URL toolbar.

Edit Links; Duplicate Links; Delete Links; Delete Unused Links

Rectangle   Circle   Polygon
URL tool   URL tool   URL tool

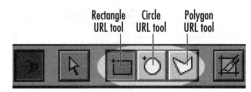

❼ *The* **URL Drawing tools**

❽ **Drag to create a URL object** *over an area of the image*

URL links are added to the different areas of an image, by drawing URL objects.

To draw a regular URL object:

1. Choose the Rectangle or Circle URL tool in the URL toolbar ❼.

2. Drag to create a rectangle or circle that defines the URL area ❽.

TIP Hold the Shift key to constrain the Rectangle to a square. (The Circle tool creates only circles, not ellipses.)

TIP Hold the Option/Alt key to drag from the center outward.

To draw a polygon URL object:

1. Choose the Polygon URL tool in the URL toolbar ❼.

2. Click to create the corner points of the polygon that defines the URL area.

❾ *The* **Show/Hide URL** *tool*

To see URL objects:

Choosing any of the URL tools automatically displays the URL objects in the image.

To hide the URLs click the Show/Hide URL tool ❾.

TIP Fireworks displays URL objects with a semitransparent color that allows you to see the URL area as well as the image underneath.

❿ *The* **URL Pointer** *tool*

You use the URL Pointer tool to modify and move URL objects.

To modify and move URL objects:

1. Choose the URL Pointer tool in the URL toolbar ❿.

2. Drag inside a URL object to move it to a new positon.

3. Drag one of the anchor points of the URL object to change its size.

Draw URL Objects; Modify and Move URL Objects

The URL objects you create take whatever link is currently visible in the URL toolbar. You can change links at any time.

To apply links to a URL object:

Select the URL object and choose a new link from the URL link list in the URL toolbar ⑪.

or

Choose Object Properties from the Panel Options of the URL toolbar. This opens the Object Properties dialog box ⑫. Then choose the link from the list.

TIP The Object Properties dialog box also allows you to change the shape of existing URL objects.

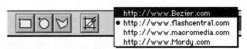

⑪ *Use the* **URL link list** *to set the URL for an object*

⑫ *Use the* **Object Properties** *dialog box to set the URL for an object or change the shape of the existing URL object.*

You do not always need to draw URL objects. Fireworks lets you copy the shape of any object and then create a URL object that exactly matches that shape. This makes it easy to align URL objects precisely to the images they cover.

To copy object shapes to URL objects:

1. Select the object you want to give a URL.

2. Choose **Select > Copy to URL** to create a URL object with the same shape.

3. Modify or change this URL object using any of the techniques in this chapter.

URL link choices

Firworks allows you to enter any sort of URL link. The three most common URL links are http, mailto, and ftp.

http stands for HyperText Transfer Protocol and is used when you want to access a Web page. For example, http://www.macromedia.com is the Web address for the Macromedia home page.

mailto is used to send e-mail. For example, mailto:Sandeec@aol.com is the URL link to send me e-mail. When your visitors click on a mailto URL it opens their browser's mail form with the proper address in the Send field.

ftp stands for File Transfer Protocol. This lets people download files. Suppose you want someone to download a document called file.sit, stored in a folder called smsc, at sandeecohen.com. The URL would be ftp://ftp.sandeecohen.com/smsc/file.sit. When your visitors click on an ftp URL it opens the file-transfer software and starts the downloading process.

SLICES 17

Why would anyone, after spending hours creating a Web graphic, want to cut it up into pieces? Well, that technique, called *slicing*, creates regions in an image that you can set to behave differently. That lets you accomplish many different effects. Because slicing is actually part of exporting, you should understand exporting (*see Chapter 15, "Basic Exporting"*) before you start this chapter.

If you used the public beta version of Fireworks available in the spring of 1998, pay careful attention to this chapter. The Fireworks engineers listened to the comments people made about how the public beta program created slices. (People were confused and did not like the limitations in the feature.) So the engineers took the time to completely redo how Fireworks creates slices.

In this chapter you will learn how to

Understand the reasons for slices.

Draw slice objects.

Set the properties for a simple sliced graphic.

Set the slice defaults.

Export a simple sliced graphic.

Set the properties for a mixed-graphic slice.

Create a text slice.

Export mixed slices.

Show or hide slice objects.

View sliced graphics in a Web browser.

Use slices in Web pages.

Why slices? (Part One)

Slices make it easier to update the images on your Web site **❶**. For instance, you might have a portion of the graphic that changes periodically. Slicing that part of the image makes it easier to update.

Sliced images also are likely to appear faster. Some Web servers can send out multiple images. So the individual slices of an image are downloaded together.

Also the first time visitors view images on the site, those images are *cached*, or stored, on their computers. So the next time visitors come to that image, even on another page, it appears faster because it is already downloaded.

Needs to be cached for many pages **Needs to be updated easily**

❶ *Disparate areas of an an image, such as standing elements and elements that must be updated frequently, such as the framed areas shown here, should be sliced.*

In order to slice a graphic, you need to draw objects that define the slice areas.

To draw slice objects:

1. Choose the Slice tool from the URL toolbar **❷**. (Be careful, it is sharp.)

2. Drag a rectangle around the area that you want to slice **❸**. This creates a slice object.

TIP The Object Properties dialog box automatically appears when you create a slice object. (*See the next exercise on how to set the Object Properties for slice objects.*)

TIP The slice tool automatically snaps to the red slice guides and edges. This avoids small gaps between slices.

3. After you have set the slice object properties, click OK and drag to create as many other slice objects as needed.

4. Use the Pointer tool in the URL toolbar to modify the size and move slice objects.

❷ *The* **Slice tool** *in the URL toolbar*

❸ *Drag the Slice tool to create a slice object*

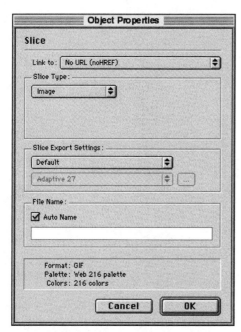

❹ *The* **Object Properties** *dialog box set for a simple slice*

Once you have created slice objects, you can then set their properties. If you are slicing an image just to make it easier to update your site or to cache certain images, you are creating a simple sliced graphic.

To set the object properties for a simple graphic:

1. Creating a slice object automatically opens the Object Properties dialog box ❹.

   TIP To set the object properties of an existing slice, select the slice and choose **Modify > Object Properties** or choose Object Properties from the URL toolbar options.

2. Choose No URL (noHREF) from the Link To list. This slices the image without assigning any image map link.

3. Choose Image from the Slice Type list.

4. Choose Default from the Slice Export Settings list. This gives the area inside the slice object the same export format as the rest of the image.

5. Check Auto Name to have Fireworks automatically name the files.

   or

   Deselect Auto Name and type your own name for the file. You do not have to add the suffix for the file format. Fireworks generates the suffix.

   TIP Naming the files yourself makes it easier for you to find the files that pertain to a specific area of the graphic.

6. Click OK to close the dialog box.

   TIP Slice objects appear as rectangles with a white tint. Each slice has a yellow border when it is not selected. Red guides indicate the other areas that are sliced.

Before you can export a sliced image, you need to set the slice defaults. These are settings used to export the entire image as either a GIF or JPEG. If you want the image to be exported as a mixtures of both GIF and JPEG images, you need to create a mixed slice (*see next page*).

To set the slice defaults:

1. Choose File > Slice Defaults. The Export Preview dialog box appears ❺.

2. Set the Export Preview as you would for any other type of graphic (*see Chapter 15, "Basic Exporting"*).

3. Click Save & Close to return to the document. This sets those export settings as the defaults for the graphic.

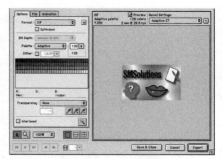

❺ *The* **Export Preview** *dialog box*

You can now export the slices for the graphic. The export command creates two files: an HTML file and the graphic slices. The HTML file contains the code necessary to assemble the slices into a table within a Web page.

To export a simple sliced graphic:

1. Choose File > Export Slices. This opens the Export dialog box.

2. Name the HTML file.

3. To create a special folder to hold all the images created in the slicing process, check Put Images in Subfolder and name the folder.

   TIP The subfolder is not necessary; it just makes it easier to deal with the many files that can be generated by slicing.

4. Click Export to create the sliced graphic.

   TIP You can check the image folder to see the separate files that are created by the slice export.

❻ *Slicing can be helpful in getting the best results for files that mix different types of images.*

Why slices? (Part Two)

Slicing also comes in handy when you need to use more than one export format for an image ❻. For instance, areas with flat art or text should be exported as GIF files, but photographs need to be saved in the JPEG format to maintain the subtleties of the image. In that case, you need to create a mixed-graphic sliced image. (This is a new feature for those who worked with the Fireworks public beta.)

You change the object properties to make a mixed-graphic slice.

To set the object properties for a mixed slice:

1. Draw the slice over the area. This automatically opens the Object Properties dialog box ❼.

2. Set the Link to No URL and the Slice Type as Image. Change the Auto Name feature as desired.

3. Choose Custom from the Slice Export Settings list. This opens another pop-up list and an ellipsis button.

4. If you have a previously saved export setting (*see page 172*), use the pop-up list to choose that setting.

5. If you do not have a preset export setting that can be used for the slice, click the ellipsis button. This opens the Export Preview dialog box.

6. Use the Export Preview box to set the format for that portion of the image and click Save & Close to return to the Object Properties box.

7. Click OK to return to the graphic.

8. Set the object properties for any other slices that require a unique format.

❼ *The* **Object Properties** *dialog box set for a custom export setting*

What if you want to add some ordinary HTML text to an area of the graphic. This makes it easy to update the information without creating new graphics. Fireworks lets you create a text slice that adds HTML text to that area of the image.

To create a text slice:

1. Draw a slice object over the area where you want the text. This automatically opens the Object Properties dialog box.

2. Set the Link to No URL.

3. Choose No Image from the Slice Type list. This opens an area where you can type HTML text ❽.

4. Type whatever text you want in the image.

TIP Use whatever HTML codes you want to set the style, color, size, and so on of the text. (For more information on the various HTML codes, see *HTML For the World Wide Web Visual Quickstart Guide* by Elizabeth Castro.)

TIP The area inside a text slice is transparent. The color seen is the document's canvas color. (*See page 21 to change the canvas color.*)

TIP You cannot see the text in a text slice in the Fireworks file. You need to export the image and view it in a Web browser ❾.

After you have set the object properties for the slice objects, you can then export the mixed sliced graphic.

To export mixed sliced graphics:

Choose **File** > **Slice Defaults** and then set the format for those areas of the image that are not covered by slice objects.

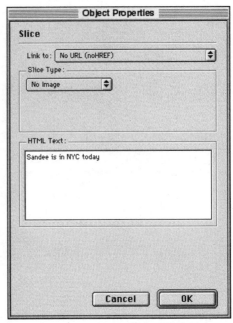

❽ *The* **Object Properties** *dialog box set for a text slice*

❾ *The results of creating a text slice as seen through a browser*

Text Slice; Export a Mixed Slice

10 *The* **Show/Hide slice** *icon in the URL toolbar*

To show and hide slice objects:

Click the Show/Hide Slice icon **10** in the URL toolbar to show or hide slice objects.

TIP You must hide slice objects before you can switch to one of the tools in the main Toolbox.

Why slices? (Part Three)

The other reason for working with slices is to create rollover buttons. Rollover buttons are covered in their own chapter. (*See Chapter 18, "Rollovers."*)

You may want to check your sliced images to make sure the slices are correct. You can easily check sliced graphics using a Web browser right on your own computer.

To view sliced graphics in a Web browser:

Drag the HTML file (FileName.htm) created by the Export Slices command onto the application icon for a browser. This opens the browser application and displays the image in the window.

TIP If the browser window is already open, you can drag the HTML file right onto the window.

To use slices in Web pages:

Once you have created the images and HTML file for a sliced graphic, you can add that HTML code to a Web page-layout program such as Dreamweaver.

TIP There are comments and instructions in the HTML file generated by Fireworks to help you add the code to programs such as Dreamweaver.

Why Slices; View Sliced Graphics; Use Slices

ROLLOVERS 18

As was mentioned earlier (*see page 191*), creating rollovers is another reason to slice images. Rollovers are like the areas on an image map: you pass your mouse over the rollover area and when you click the mouse you are taken to a new Web page. However, image maps give you only a little feedback as you pass your mouse over the area. Rollovers can give you all sorts of visual feedback when you pass you mouse over the area, when you click on the area, and when you release the mouse. The added visual feedback gives more enjoyment to people visiting a site.

Some people use the term buttons instead of rollovers. This is because many rollover images look like buttons that you press to move to a link. This chapter uses the term rollover, rather than button.

In this chapter you will learn how to:

Understand what the rollover states do.

Use the frame panel to create the rollover images.

Use the bevel presets to create a pressed button.

Create multiple rollovers.

Copy objects to frames.

Create the slice object for a rollover.

Set the object properties for rollover slice objects.

Set the slice defaults for rollovers.

Export rollovers.

Use the Demo Rollover HTML.

macromedia
FIREWORKS

When you define image maps as clickable areas, you give visitors to your Web page only a very subtle hint that they can click there: the cursor changes as it passes over links in the image ❶. Rollovers give the image itself a visual cue depending on the position or action of the mouse ❷. The different rollover states ❸ can help users figure out more quickly how to use your site. Rollovers can also make it more fun to use the elements in your site. Fireworks makes it easy to create the rollover images as well as the HTML code necessary to run the rollovers.

The four rollover states:

- **Plain image** is the look of the image when there is no mouse inside the image. This is the regular state of the rollover image area.

- **Over** is the look of the image when the mouse has passed over the rollover area. This look gives the viewer feedback that this area responds to mouse actions.

- **Down** is the look of the image when the mouse is released after clicking the rollover. This state is actually seen only on the destination Web page, that is, the page to which the button links. The down state comes from Frame 3 of the export of the rollover image.

- **onClick** is the look of the image when the mouse button is pressed. This is the look that is seen as the browser switches to the linked page. The onClick state comes from Frame 4 of the export of the rollover image. Because this state is seen so briefly, it is rarely used by Web designers.

❶ *When the mouse **passes over an image map**, it shows a simple hand cursor.*

❷ *When the mouse **passes over a rollover**. it shows the hand cursor and whatever image was created for the Over state. In this case a glow was added for the Over state.*

❸ *The **four rollover states** can be set for whatever looks you want. Each state gives a different cue for the action of the mouse.*

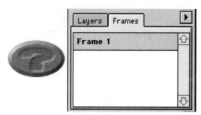

❹ *The* **Frames panel** *creates the different rollover states.*

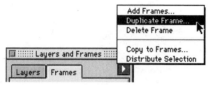

❺ *The* **Duplicate Frames** *command in the Frames panel menu*

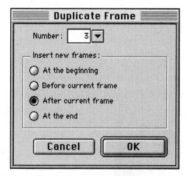

❻ *The* **Duplicate Frame** *dialog box*

You make rollovers by duplicating the images on frames and then making changes to reflect each of the rollover states on each of the frames. Each frame of the image controls a different rollover state.

To use the frame panel to create rollover images:

1. Draw the object for the basic rollover state. Add text if necessary.

2. Open the Frames panel by choosing **Window > Frames**.

   or

   Click the Frames panel tab to switch from the Layers panel to the Frames panel ❹.

3. Choose Duplicate Frame from the Frames panel pop-up list ❺ to open the Duplicate Frame dialog box ❻.

4. In order to have three more rollover states, adjust the slider control or use the field to enter the number 3.

5. Check to insert the new frames after the current frame.

6. Click OK. Three additional frames appear in the Frames panel ❼. After you create additional frames, frame 2 becomes the current frame.

TIP The four frames you have just created are all identical. They now need to be modified to show different looks in the rollover.

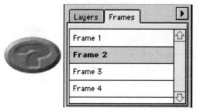

❼ *Duplicate frames appear in the* **Frames panel**

The rollover states are usually created to mimic the look of a button being pressed. Fireworks has presets in the Effect panel that make it very easy to create that look. (*See page 107 for more information on the Bevel Presets.*)

To use the bevel presets to create a pressed button:

1. Create an object and give it an inner or outer bevel effect.

2. Use the steps in the previous exercise to duplicate the first frame onto three additional frames.

3. Click Frame 1 to make that frame active and select the object on that frame.

4. Set the button preset list to Raised ❽. (Raised leaves the object as originally styled ❾.)

5. Activate Frame 2 and select the object on that frame. Then change the button preset to Highlight ❽. (This lightens the objects as if a 25% white tint were applied over it ❾.)

6. Activate Frame 3 and select the object on that frame. Then change the button preset to Inset ❽. (This reverses the lighting of the bevel to invert the 3D effect ❾.)

7. Activate Frame 4 and select the object on that frame. Then change the button preset to Invert ❽. (This reverses the lighting and lightens the object with a tint ❾.)

TIP You do not need to use the bevel presets to create rollovers. Any effects can be used. For instance, you can use drop shadows and glows to create the effect of a floating button that is pushed down closer to the background of the page ❿.

Bevel Presets

❽ *The* bevel presets *list*

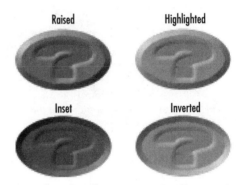

❾ *The* **four bevel presets** *applied to an oval button with an inner bevel*

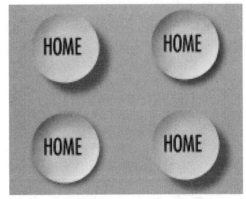

❿ *An example of how the four rollover states can be used to create the look of a button that moves down and up as the user "presses" it.*

① Multiple objects *can be created for multiple rollovers.*

The image in the previous exercise is good for a single rollover but most of the time you need more than one button on a page. You might want to have a series of buttons that direct visitors to different places on your Web site. Rather than make a single rollover again and again, you can easily create multiple rollover images at once.

To create multiple rollovers:

1. Create the object for the first rollover image.

2. Hold the Option/Alt key and drag that image to the position for the next rollover image.

3. If desired, change the appearance of this object.

4. Repeat steps 2 and 3 to make as many objects as you need **①**.

5. Choose Duplicate Frame from the Frames panel to make 3 additional frames each containing the multiple images.

6. Select each frame in the Frames panel to make whatever changes you want for the objects on each frame.

Multiple Rollovers

You may need to add an object to all the frames. For instance, you might want to add text to objects that have already been duplicated onto frames. Fortunately, you can copy objects to frames.

To copy objects to frames:

1. Use the file you created in the previous exercise. (This is several objects duplicated onto four frames.)

2. Select Frame 1 and type some text over one of the objects.

3. Option/Alt-drag the text to copy it to the other objects in that frame. Change the text over the other objects.

4. Select all the text objects and use the Frames panel list to choose Copy to Frames ⓬. The Copy to Frames dialog box appears ⓭.

5. Choose All frames and then click OK. The selected text objects are copied to all four frames.

TIP After you have copied the objects to all four frames, you need to move to each frame and modify the objects to the look of each rollover state.

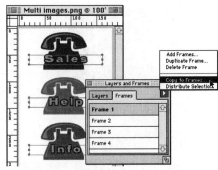

⓬ Use **Copy to Frames** to copy selected items to all the frames of a document.

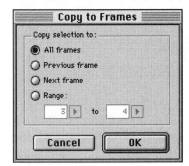

⓭ The **Copy to Frames** dialog box

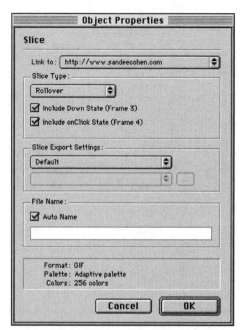

⓮ *The* **Object Properties** *dialog box set for a Rollover slice object.*

Once you have created the images for a rollover, you then need to create a slice object to define the area as a rollover.

To create the slice object for a rollover:

1. Choose the Slice tool from the Image Map toolbar. (*See Chapter 17, "Slices" for working with the Slice tool.*)

2. With any of the frames active, drag a slice object rectangle that defines the area of the rollover. The Object Properties dialog box for the slice object appears. (*See the next exercise on how to set the object properties of a slice.*)

3. After you have set the object properties for the slice, you can create slices for other rollovers.

TIP Hold the Option/Alt key and drag the slice object to copy the slice object.

The object properties for the slices need to be defined as rollovers in order to generate the multiple images for a rollover.

To set the object properties for a rollover area:

1. Select the slice object for the rollover.

2. Choose **Modify** > **Object Properties** to open the Object Properties dialog box **⓮**.

3. Set the Link to for the slice. This is the Web page that the rollover sends the viewer to.

4. Set the Slice Type to Rollover.

5. Check Include Down State to include the information on frame 3.

6. Check Include onClick State to include the information on frame 4.

7. Set the Slice Export Settings to Default or Custom. (*See page 189 for how to set the Custom options.*)

8. Click OK to apply the object properties for the slice object.

As discussed in chapter 17, the default slice format is the format used for those objects set in the Object Properties to Default (*see the previous exercise*). It is also the format used for those areas of the image that are not covered by a slice. (*For more information on exporting, see Chapter 15, "Basic Exporting" and Chapter 17, "Slices."*)

To set the slice defaults:

1. Choose **File > Slice Defaults**. The Export Preview dialog box appears.

2. Set the export format controls in the Export Preview window as you would for any other type of graphics.

TIP You cannot set slice defaults as Animated GIF, GIF Rollover, or JPEG Rollover 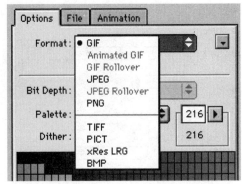. This is because rollover properties are set by the Object Properties of the slice object (*see the previous page*), not the export format. For a GIF rollover, you should choose GIF. For a JPEG rollover, you should choose JPEG.

3. Click Save & Close to return to the document. This sets the settings as the defaults for slices.

TIP Use Custom if the rollover image needs a special export setting.

⓯ *The **Export Slices** dialog box*

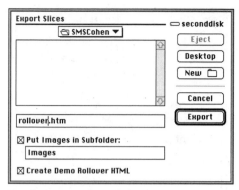

⑯ *The* **Export Slices** *dialog box*

Once you have created the slice objects and set the slice defaults, you can then export the slices for the rollover.

To export a rollover:

1. Choose **File** > **Export Slices**. This opens the Export Slices dialog box **⑯**.
2. Name the HTML file.
3. To create a special folder to hold all the images created in the slicing process, check Put Images in Subfolder, and name the folder.

TIP The subfolder is not necessary; it just makes it easier to deal with the many files that can be generated by slicing.

4. Check Demo Rollover HTML to create a demo version of the HTML code that you can use to test your rollover without creating a complete Web site or posting the rollover onto a server.
5. Click OK to generate the HTML code and images for the rollover.

One of the challenges to creating rollovers is that you need to move to the destination page to see if the Down state has been created correctly. Rather than post the rollovers on an actual Web site, Fireworks lets you create a demo version of your rollover. This demo version lets you see how the rollover works.

To use the Demo Rollover HTML:

1. Drag the file FileName_demo.htm onto a browser application or window. The rollover appears in the browser window 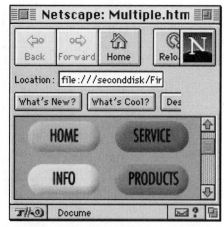.

2. Move the mouse over the rollover. The image changes to the Over state.

3. Click the rollover. The image changes to the onClick state and then switches to the Down state.

TIP You can also use the HTML code generated by the Demo as code that can be updated and used for various rollovers in different Web pages.

⑰ *The **Demo Rollover HTML** code lets you see the four states of a rollover in the browser window.*

ANIMATIONS | 19

It is hard to believe that just a few years ago, there were very few Web pages with animated images. Now, so many Web images move, change from one shape to another, and do other simple animations. Fireworks gives you all the tools you need to create these simple animations. (Animations from Fireworks are called simple animations to distinguish them from the more sophisticated animations created by programs such as Flash and Dreamweaver.)

In this chapter you will learn how to

Open the Frames panel.

Distribute objects onto frames.

Copy objects onto frames.

Use layers with frames.

Distribute vector layers onto frames.

Distribute vector pages onto frames.

Create symbols and instances.

Modify symbols and instances.

Create motion by tweening.

Create transformations by tweening.

Create fades by tweening.

Set the animation export controls.

Set the timing of an animation.

Set the disposal of an animtion.

Set the number of times an animation plays.

Preview animations.

Export animations.

Any animation—cartoon, Web graphic, or motion picture—is basically a series of still images that appears quickly, giving the illusion of motion. (Just like the flip books you played with as a child.) In Fireworks each one of those still images is created using the Frames panel.

To open the Frames panel:

Choose **Windows** > **Frames** or click the Frames tab of the Layers and Frames panel. The Frames panel appears ❶.

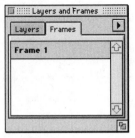

❶ *The* Frames panel

If you have several different Fireworks objects you can easily put them on individual frames to create a simple animation.

To distribute objects onto frames:

1. Create a file with several different objects on Frame 1.

2. Select all the objects and choose Distribute Selection from the Frames panel ❷. New frames are created with each of the objects in the selection on its own frame ❸.

TIP The number of objects determines the number of frames.

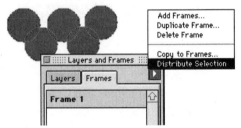

❷ *The* **Distribute Selection** *command*

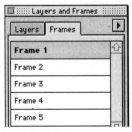

❸ *Choosing Distribute Selection sends each of the original objects onto its own frame.*

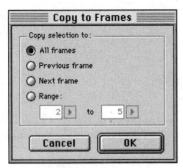

④ *The* **Copy to Frames** *dialog box*

You might also want one object to appear throughout all frames of an animation. For instance, you might want to have text that appears next to all the objects in the animation. This is accomplished by copying the text onto the frames.

To copy objects onto frames:

1. Use the file you created in the previous exercise and create some text on Frame 1. Make sure to position the text so that it will not overlap any of the objects on the other frames.

TIP It is important that the text not overlap the original objects because objects copied onto frames are copied in front of the objects that already exist on the frames.

2. With the text selected, choose Copy to frames from the Frames panel menu. The Copy to Frames dialog box appears **④**.

3. Choose All frames to copy the selected text onto all the frames of the image.

TIP Use the other selections in the Copy to Frames dialog box to copy an object to a specific frame or a range of frames.

Copy Objects onto Frames

Positioning the text apart from the objects solved the layering problem in the previous exercise. What if you must create an object that fits behind all the other objects in frames? Fortunately, you can use layers to control the order of objects copied to frames.

To use layers with frames:

1. Use the file you created in the previous exercise and click the Layers tab of the Layers and Frames panel.

2. Choose New Layer from the Layers panel menu **❺**. The Add Layer dialog box appears.

3. Name the layer and click OK. This creates a new layer positioned at the top of the Layers panel.

4. Drag the layer you just created below the Foreground layer **❻**.

5. Add an object that covers most of the image to this layer.

TIP Because the new layer is positioned *behind* the other layer, this object can overlap any of the other objects in the animations.

6. With the object still selected, switch to the Frames panel and choose Copy to Frames. The new object is duplicated to all the frames, but because it is on a layer positioned behind the foreground layer, the object stays behind all the original objects **❼**.

TIP Moving the layer in the Layers panel changes the position of the object on all the frames.

TIP Any images on the Background layer are visible on all the frames of a document.

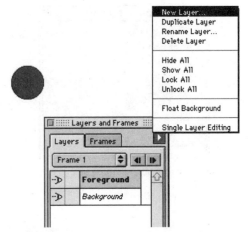

❺ *The* **New Layer** *command*

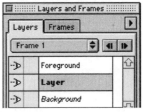

❻ **Moving a layer below another** *allows the objects on that layer to be seen behind the objects on layers above.*

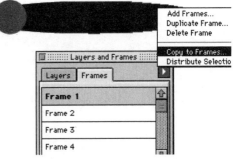

❼ **Copy the object to frames** *allows the object to be seen throughout the animation.*

Use Layers

Frame Previous Next
list frame frame

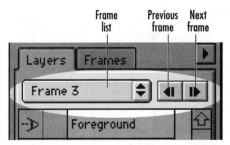

❽ *The* **Frame controls** *in the Layers panel*

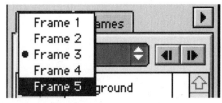

❾ *The* **Frame list** *in the Layers panel*

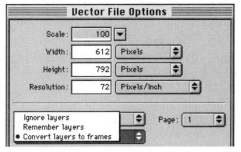

❿ *The* **Layers pop-up list** *lets you move objects from layers to frames.*

⓫ *Assigning a blend to layers in FreeHand and then importing the art into Fireworks allows you to* **create an animation** *of one letter turning into another.*

You may find it awkward to be constantly switching between the Layers panel and the Frame panel. Fireworks lets you control frames while still in the Layers panel.

To control frames in the Layers panel:

1. Switch to the Layers panel.

2. Click the Next frame or Previous frame buttons ❽ to move from one frame to the next one. The Frame list shows you what frame you are on.

 or

 Use the Frame list to jump from one frame to another, bypassing the frames in between ❾.

Although Fireworks has a robust set of drawing tools, it lacks some other useful features, such as blends, that are found only in programs such as Macromedia FreeHand and Adobe Illustrator. Fortunately, you can turn the layers and pages from vector programs into Fireworks frames.

To distribute vector layers onto frames:

1. Choose **File** >**Import** and find a vector file with objects on separate layers. This opens the Vector File Options dialog box.

TIP FreeHand's Animate Xtra makes it easy to create a blend and then send each object of the blend to its own layer.

2. Use the Layers pop-up list ❿ to assign objects on each layer to frames and then click the OK button.

3. Use the animation export settings (*see pages 241–217*) to animate the objects on each frame ⓫.

Control Frames in Layers Panel; Distribute Vector Layers

You can also use FreeHand's multiple pages to create animations in Fireworks. This gives you different options than working with objects on layers.

To distribute pages onto frames:

1. Choose File>Import and find a vector file with objects on separate pages. This opens the Vector File Options dialog box.

2. Use the Pages pop-up list ⑩ to assign objects on each page to frames and then click the OK button.

3. Use the animation export settings (*see pages 214–217*) to animate the objects on each frame.

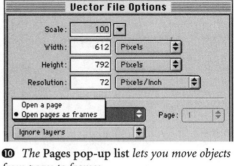

⑩ *The* **Pages pop-up list** *lets you move objects from pages to frames.*

Copying objects to frames helps create animations, but what if you then needed to change the look of the object? To open each frame individually and make the changes would be a very laborious process. Fireworks lets you have one object control the appearance of others. This is called *symbols* and *instances*.

⑪ *A* **Symbol,** *designated by the plus sign in the corner*

To create a symbol:

1. Select the object or objects that you want to be the symbol.

2. Choose **Edit**>**Symbols**>**Make Symbol.** A plus sign appears in the bottom corner of the image ⑪ that indicates the object is a symbol.

Distributes Pages; Create a Symbol

⓬ Pasting an instance *positions it so that it covers the symbol*

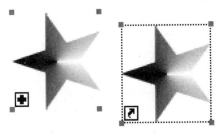

⓭ Holding the Option/Alt key *as you drag a symbol creates an instance of the symbol.*

Instances are simply objects created from symbols. There are several ways to create an instance based on a symbol.

To copy and paste an instance from a symbol:

1. Copy the symbol.

2. Paste. The instance covers the symbol. A small arrow in the corner of the object indicates it is an instance **⓬**.

TIP If you switch to a new frame before you paste, the instance is pasted directly over the symbol but in the new frame.

3. Move the instance to wherever you want it to be.

4. Repeat steps 2 and 3 to create as many instances as needed.

TIP You do not have to copy the original symbol to create an instance. Instances can be copied from other instances.

To Option/Alt-drag an instance from a symbol:

1. Select the symbol

2. Hold the Option/Alt key as you drag the symbol. The copy created is an instance **⓭**.

3. Repeat to create as many instances as needed.

TIP Instances copied from other instances are based on the original symbol.

You can also create instances by using the frame commands. This automatically creates instances on the other frames.

To create instances onto frames:

1. Select the symbol.

2. Switch to the Frames panel and choose Copy to Frames. Instances based on that symbol are created on all the frames.

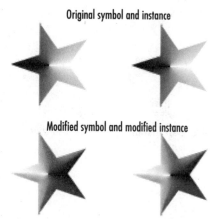

Original symbol and instance

Modified symbol and modified instance

Once you have created a symbol with instances, you can modify the symbol to change the appearance of its instances.

To modify symbols and instances:

Select the symbol and change its appearance. All instances of that symbol change accordingly ⓴.

⓴ Modifying a symbol

To change the shape of symbols and instances:

Select the symbol with the Subselection tool and modify its anchor points. All instances of that symbol change accordingly ⓯.

⓯ **Moving the points of a symbol** *changes the point in the instance.*

To move both the symbol and instances:

Move the symbol with the Subselection tool. All instances of that symbol move accordingly.

To move only the symbol:

Move the symbol with the Pointer tool. The symbol moves without affecting the position of its instances.

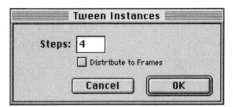

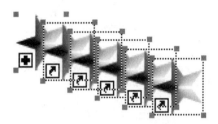

⓰ *The* Tween Instances *dialog box*

⓱ *The results of* tweening between a symbol and its instance

Once you have a symbol and an instance, you can create other instances between the two. This is called *tweening*. In tweening, each new instance changes from the original symbol until it becomes the final instance. This is similar to the blend command in print graphics.

When a symbol in one position and its instance in another are tweened, it results in a series of identical instances spaced in between. All of the objects can then be used to create motion in an animation.

To create motion by tweening:

1. Position the symbol where you want the move to start.

2. Position the instance where you want the move to end.

3. Select both the symbol and instance, and choose **Edit > Symbols > Tween Instances**. The Tween Instances dialog box appears ⓰.

4. Set the number of new instances in the Steps field.

5. Click Distribute to Frames to automatically create new frames with each instance on its own frame.

   TIP If you do not distribute the instances to frames with the Tween Instances dialog box, you can still use the Distribute Selection command from the Frames panel (*see page 204*) to create the animation later. This lets you judge to see if you like the position of all the tweened objects.

6. Click OK. The new instances fill in the space between the original symbol and its instance ⓱.

Symbols and instances do not have to look identical. You can transform the shape of an instance without changing the symbol. Tweening between a transformed instance and its symbol creates an animation in which an object transforms, or morphs, from one shape into another.

To create transformations by tweening:

1. Position the symbol where you want the transformation to start.

2. Position the instance where you want the transformation to end.

3. Use the Scale, Rotation, or Perspective tools to change the appearance of the instance (*see page 67–71*).

TIP The Distortion tool does not create transformations between symbols and instances.

4. Select both the symbol and instance, and choose **Edit > Symbols > Tween Instances**.

5. Set the number of new instances in the Steps field.

6. Click Distribute to Frames to automatically create new frames with each instance on its own frame.

TIP If you do not distribute the instances to frames with the Tween Instances dialog box, you can still use the Distribute Selection command from the Frames panel (*see page 204*) to create the animation later.

7. Click OK. The tweened instances morph from one object to another **⑱**.

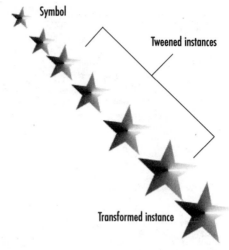

⑱ *The results of* tweening between a symbol and a transformed instance

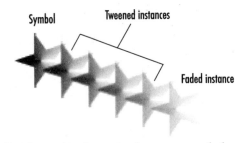

Symbol Tweened instances

Faded instance

19 *The results of* tweening between a symbol and a faded instance

You can also modify the opacity of an instance. Tweening then creates an animation in which one object fades in or out.

To create fades by tweening:

1. Position the symbol where you want the fade to start.
2. Position the instance where you want the fade to end.
3. Change the opacity of the instance.
4. Select both the symbol and instance, and choose **Edit** > **Symbols** > **Tween Instances**.
5. Set the number of steps, Distribute to Frames as desired, and click OK. The tweened instances fade from one object to another **19**.

Several other commands are useful for working with symbols and instances. For instance, you may find that you need to add another object to the ones originally created as a symbol.

To add objects to the symbol:

Select the original symbol and the objects you want to add to it and choose **Edit** > **Symbols** > **Add to Symbol**. The new object joins the symbol and any instances based on that symbol.

To break the link between a symbol and its instance:

Select the instance from a symbol choose **Edit** > **Symbols** > **Break Link**. The instance is released and appears as an ordinary object.

TIP The Break Link command allows you to make refinements to objects used as part of an animation.

Fade by Tweening; Add Objects; Break Links

To find the symbol an instance is based on:

Select the instance and choose **Edit** > **Symbols** >**Find Symbol**. The symbol is selected.

TIP The Find Symbol command works even if the instance is on one frame and the symbol is on another.

To delete the instances based on a symbol:

Select the symbol and choose **Edit** > **Symbols** >**Delete Instances**. All the instances based on that symbol are deleted.

TIP The Delete Instances command does not delete the frames that held the instances.

Placing the objects on frames is only half of creating animations. You need to adjust several other settings.

To set the animation export controls:

1. Choose **File** >**Export** to open the Export Preview window 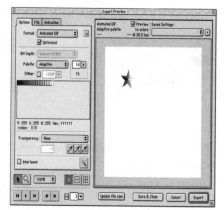.

2. Choose Animated GIF from the Format list.

3. Set the GIF color options as desired (*see Chapter 15, "Basic Exporting."*)

4. Click the Animation tab in the Export Preview window to open the animation options 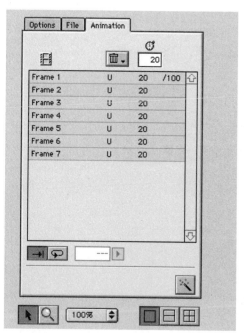.

⑳ *The* **Export Preview** *dialog box for a GIF animation*

㉑ *The* **Animation options** *of the Export Preview*

Frame delay field

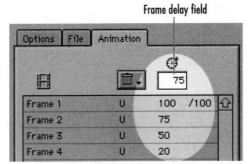

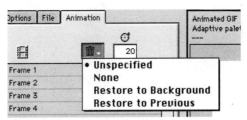

㉒ *Set the* **timing amount** *to control how long a specific frame is visible during an animation.*

㉓ *The* **Disposal method** *list*

The animation options let you control the timing for each of the frames of the animation.

To set the timing of an animation:

1. Select a frame in the animation options.

2. Enter a number in the frame delay field **㉒**. This is set in hundredths of a second. The higher the number, the longer the frame is visible.

TIP Use the Shift key to select more than one frame at a time.

You can also control how each frame blends between other frames and the background. This is called the disposal of the frames.

To set the disposal of frames:

1. Select a frame in the animation options.

2. Use the Disposal method list **㉓** to control how Fireworks treats the disposal of one frame to another.

- Choose **Unspecified** when there is no transparency in the animation. If Unspecified is turned on with a transparency, instead of each frame changing from one to another, each frame is added to the image.

- Choose **None** to add some of the image in the next frame to the previous one.

- Choose **Restore to Background** when transparency is turned on so that each frame changes from one to another.

- Choose **Revert to Background** when moving objects appear over a larger frame that appeared earlier in the animation. Since Revert to Background is not supported by all browsers, use it with restraint.

Timing: Disposal of Frames

You can also set how many times the animation plays.

To set the number of times the animation plays:

1. Set the Loop control ❷❹ to either Play Once or Loop. (*Loop* means the animation repeats.)

2. If you choose Loop, set how many times the animation is repeated.

- Choose a number to repeat the animation a finite number of times.

- Choose Forever to repeat the animation for as long as the viewer stays on the page.

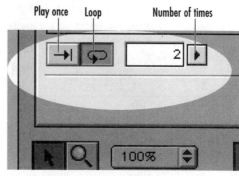

❷❹ *The Loop controls*

Once you have created an animation, you can preview it within Fireworks to see if it is correct. This is done with the player controls ❷❺.

To preview animations:

1. Click the Play/Stop button to start the animation. The animation plays as many times as specified in the Loop controls.

2. Click the Play/Stop button to stop an animation that is playing. The animation stops on whatever frame is active.

3. Click the First Frame button to "rewind" the animation to the beginning.

4. Click the Last Frame button to skip to the end of the animation.

5. Click the Previous or Next Frame buttons to move one frame at a time.

6. Use the Frame slider to skip to a specific frame in the animation.

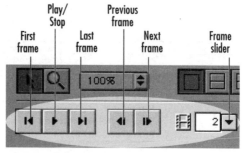

❷❺ *The player controls*

Once you have set the controls for the animation, you can then export it.

To export animations:

1. In the Export Preview window, click Export.

2. Give the file a name and then click OK. The file is saved as a GIF animation file, which can be incorporated into a Web page.

DEFAULTS

As you have seen, Fireworks provides a great number of preset patterns, gradients, brushes, and effects that you can apply to objects. You can modify the default settings to create other effects. (Just remember the immortal words, "Defaults, dear Brutus, lie not in our stars, but in our software.")

This appendix shows the default settings for the presets. In each case, consider the defaults as just the start for creating your own looks.

In Appendix A you will see printouts of

> The textures used for fills and brushes.
> The patterns at their default settings.
> The gradients at their default settings.
> The brushes at their default settings.
> The effects at their default settings.

macromedia
FIREWORKS

Textures

The 26 textures can be applied to either fills or brushes. Once the textures are applied, they can then be adjusted using the opacity slider.

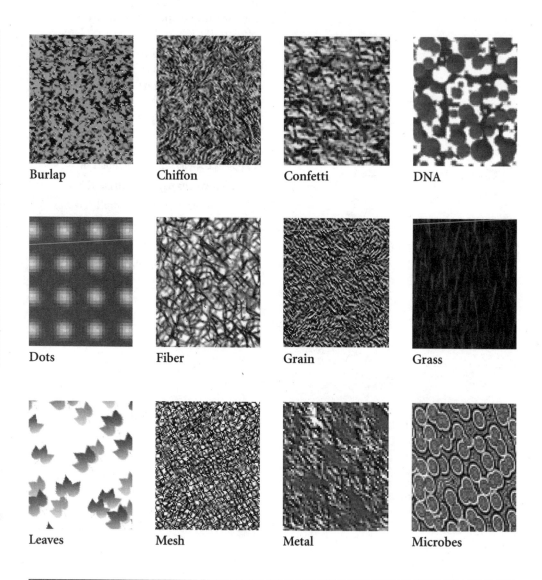

Burlap   Chiffon   Confetti   DNA

Dots   Fiber   Grain   Grass

Leaves   Mesh   Metal   Microbes

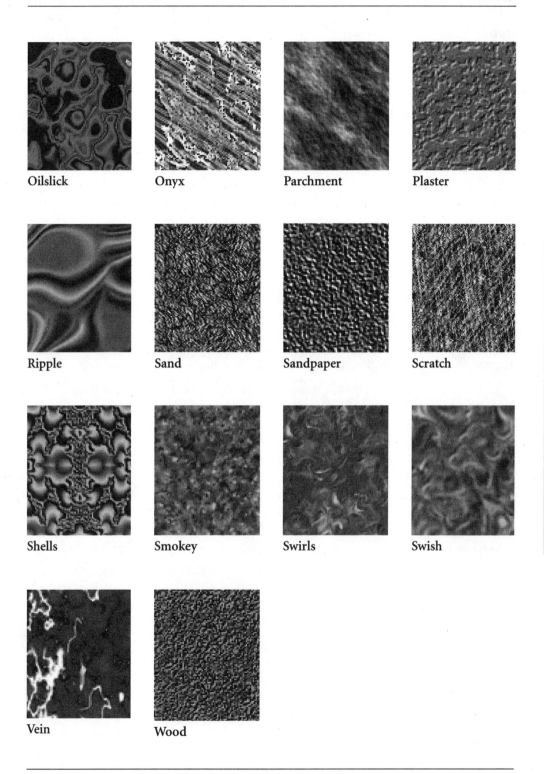

Oilslick   Onyx   Parchment   Plaster

Ripple   Sand   Sandpaper   Scratch

Shells   Smokey   Swirls   Swish

Vein   Wood

Textures

Patterns

The 14 patterns can be applied as fills. Once the patterns have been applied, they can then be adjusted using the Paint Bucket. These are the patterns in the order they appear in the patterns list.

Aggregate   Bark   Berber Rug   Blue Wave

Bricks-Small   Grass-Tiny   Illusion   Impressionist-Red

Jeans

Leaves-Photinia

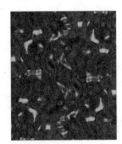

Red Goo

Tweed

Weave

Wood-Light

Gradients

The 11 gradients can be applied as fills.
Once the gradients have been applied, you
can adjust them using the Paint Bucket.
These are the gradients in the order they
appear in the gradients list.

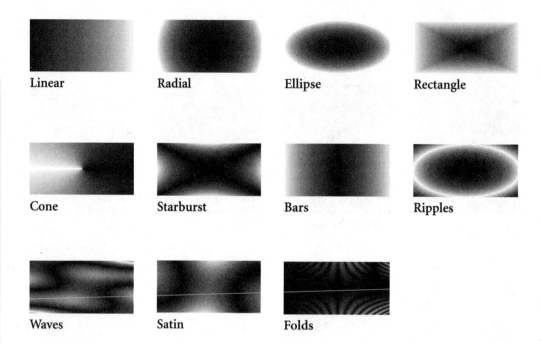

Linear   Radial   Ellipse   Rectangle

Cone   Starburst   Bars   Ripples

Waves   Satin   Folds

Brushes

You can apply the 48 brushes to open or closed paths. Once the brushes have been applied, you can then adjust them using the Brushes panel.

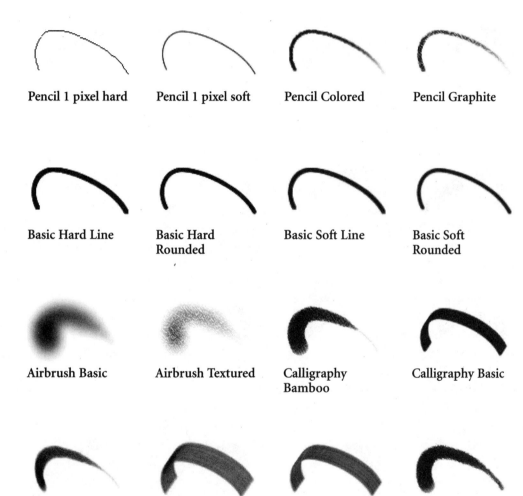

Pencil 1 pixel hard	Pencil 1 pixel soft	Pencil Colored	Pencil Graphite
Basic Hard Line	Basic Hard Rounded	Basic Soft Line	Basic Soft Rounded
Airbrush Basic	Airbrush Textured	Calligraphy Bamboo	Calligraphy Basic
Calligraphy Quill	Calligraphy Ribbon	Calligraphy Wet	Charcoal Creamy

Brushes

Brushes (continued)

Charcoal Pastel   Charcoal Textured   Charcoal Soft   Crayon Basic

Crayon Rake   Crayon Thick   Felt Tip
Dark Marker   Felt Tip
Highlighter

Felt Tip
Light Marker   Felt Tip Thin   Oil Bristle   Oil Broad Splatter

Oil Splatter   Oil Strands   Oil Textured
Bristles   Watercolor Heavy

Watercolor Thick   Watercolor Thin   Random Confetti   Random Dots

Random Fur   Random Squares   Random Yarn   Unnatural 3D

Unnatural 3D   Unnatural   Unnatural Fluid   Unnatural Outline
Glow   Chameleon   Splatter

Unnatural Paint   Unnatural   Unnatural Toxic   Unnatural Viscous
Splatter   Toothpaste   Waste   Alien Paint

Brushes

Effects

You can apply the 20 effects to vector objects or pixel images. Once the textures are applied, you can adjust them using the Effects panel. The effects shown here are in the order they appear in the Effect panel. They have been applied to the same object. Any differences in the sizes are a result of applying the effects.

Inner Bevel Flat	Inner Bevel Frame 1	Inner Bevel Frame 2	Inner Bevel Ring
Inner Bevel Ruffle	Inner Bevel Smooth	Inner Bevel Sloped	Outer Bevel Flat
Outer Bevel Frame 1	Outer Bevel Frame 2	Outer Bevel Ring	Outer Bevel Ruffle
Outer Bevel Sloped	Outer Bevel Smooth	Drop Shadow Basic	Drop Shadow Soft
Embossed Inset	Embossed Raised	Glow Basic	Glow Halo

KEYBOARD SHORTCUTS B

A s you become more familiar with the various Fireworks features, you should begin to use the keyboard shortcuts for the commands you use most often. For instance, rather than use the mouse to choose **File > Export,** it is much faster and easier to use the keyboard shortcut.

This appendix lists the shortcuts for Fireworks menu commands. Most of these shortcuts are listed on the menus. So you do not have to use this list to find the shortuct for the commands you use the most. However, this list can make it easy to find a certain shortcut, or even to tell if a command has a shortcut assigned to it.

In Appendix B you have

A list of the keyboard shortcuts for the Windows platform on pages 230–231.

A list of the keyboard shortcuts for the Macintosh platform on pages 232–233.

A list of the keyboard shortcuts to access the tools in the Toolbox on pages 234.

WINDOWS KEYBOARD SHORTCUTS

The following are the keyboard shortcuts for the Windows platform. These are the abbreviations used for the keys.

Ctrl	Ctrl key
Alt	Alt key
Up	Up arrow key
Down	Down arrow key
Left	Left arrow key
Right	Right arrow key
Space	Spacebar

File Menu (Win)

New	Ctrl+N
Open	Ctrl+O (oh)
Print	Ctrl+P
Quit	Ctrl+Q
Import	Ctrl+R
Close Window	Ctrl+W
Export	Ctrl+Shift+R
Save	Ctrl+S
Save As	Ctrl+Shift+S

Select Menu (Win)

Copy to URL	Ctrl+Shift+U
Select All	Ctrl+A
Deselect (Select None)	Ctrl+D
Inverse	Ctrl+Shift+I
Convert to Image	Ctrl+Alt+Shift+Z
Superselect	Ctrl+Up
Subselect	Ctrl+Down

View Menu (Win)

Show All	Ctrl+Shift+M
Hide Selection	Ctrl+M
Hide Edges	Ctrl+H
Full Display/Draft Toggle	Ctrl+K
Fit Selection	Ctrl+0 (zero)
100% Magnification	Ctrl+1
200% Magnification	Ctrl+2
400% Magnification	Ctrl+4
50% Magnification	Ctrl+5
800% Magnification	Ctrl+8
3200% Magnification	Ctrl+3
6400% Magnification	Ctrl+6
Show/Hide Rulers	Ctrl+Alt+R
Fit All	Ctrl+Alt+0 (zero)
Zoom Out	Ctrl+-
Zoom In	Ctrl++
Zoom In tool	Ctrl+space
Zoom Out tool	Ctrl+Alt+space

Edit Menu (Win)

Copy	Ctrl+C
Clone	Ctrl+Shift+C
Ungroup	Ctrl+U
Paste	Ctrl+V
Cut	Ctrl+X
Undo	Ctrl+Z
Paste Inside	Ctrl+Shift+V
Crop Selected Image	Ctrl+Alt+C
Edit Grid dialog	Ctrl+Alt+G
Create Empty Image (tool)	Ctrl+Alt+Y
Redo	Ctrl+ Shift + Z
Edit Guides dialog	Ctrl+Alt+Shift+G
Paste Attributes	Ctrl+Alt+Shift+V

Modify Menu (Win)

Edit Image Object. . . . Ctrl+Shift+O (oh)

Edit Background Image . . . . Ctrl+E

Bring to Front . . . . Ctrl+F

Send to Back . . . . Ctrl+B

Group . . . . Ctrl+G

Object Properties . . . . Ctrl+I

Join . . . . Ctrl+J

Transform. . . . . Ctrl+T

Rotate 90° CCW. . . . . Ctrl+7

Rotate 90° CW. . . . . Ctrl+9

Send Backward . . . . Ctrl+Shift+B

Exit Image Edit Mode. . . . . Ctrl+Shift+D

Bring Forward . . . . Ctrl+Shift+F

Mask Group . . . . Ctrl+Shift+G

Split. . . . . Ctrl+Shift+J

Align Objects Left. . . . . Ctrl+Alt+2

Align Objects Center/Vert. . . . Ctrl+Alt+3

Align Objects Right. . . . . . . Ctrl+Alt+4

Align Objects Top . . . . Ctrl+Alt+5

Align Objects Center/Horiz. . . Ctrl+Alt+6

Align Objects Bottom . . . . . Ctrl+Alt+7

Distribute Widths. . . . . Ctrl+Alt+8

Distribute Heights . . . . Ctrl+Alt+9

Text Menu (Win)

Text Editor . . . . Ctrl+Shift+E

Convert to Paths . . . . Ctrl+Shift+P

Attach Text to Path . . . . . . Ctrl+Shift+Y

Bold Text . . . . Ctrl+Alt+Shift+B

Center-Align Text. . . . . Ctrl+Alt+Shift+C

Italic Text . . . . Ctrl+Alt+Shift+I

Justify Text. . . . . Ctrl+Alt+Shift+J

Left-Align Text. . . . . . . Ctrl+Alt+Shift+L

Bold-Italic Text. . . Ctrl+Alt+Shift+O (oh)

Plain Text . . . . Ctrl+Alt+Shift+P

Right-Align Text . . . . . Ctrl+Alt+Shift+R

Stretch-Justify Text . . . . Ctrl+Alt+Shift+S

Window Menu (Win)

Brush panel. . . . . Ctrl+Alt+B

Effect panel. . . . . Ctrl+Alt+E

Fill panel . . . . Ctrl+Alt+F

Frames panel. . . . . Ctrl+Alt+K

Layers panel . . . . Ctrl+Alt+L

Color Mixer panel . . . . Ctrl+Alt+M

New Window . . . . Ctrl+Alt+N

Tool Options panel . . . . Ctrl+Alt+O (oh)

Info panel . . . . Ctrl+Alt+I

Opacity panel . . . . Ctrl+Alt+P

Swatches panel. . . . . Ctrl+Alt+S

Toolbox . . . . Ctrl+Alt+T

URLs panel. . . . . Ctrl+Alt+U

Xtras (Win)

Repeat Xtra. . . . . Ctrl+Alt+Shift+X

MACINTOSH KEYBOARD SHORTCUTS

The following are the keyboard shortcuts for the Macintosh platform. These are the abbreviations used for the keys.

Cmd . . . . Command key
Opt . . . . Option key
Up. . . . . Up arrow key
Down . . . . Down arrow key
Left. . . . . Left arrow key
Right . . . . Right arrow key
Space . . . . Spacebar

File Menu (Mac)

New. . . . . Cmd+N
Open. . . . . Cmd+O (oh)
Print . . . . Cmd+P
Quit . . . . Cmd+Q
Import . . . . Cmd+R
Export . . . . Cmd+Shift+R
Close Window. . . . . Cmd+W
Save . . . . Cmd+S
Save As . . . . Cmd+Shift+S

Select Menu (Mac)

Copy to URL. . . . . Cmd+Shift+U
Select All. . . . . Cmd+A
Deselect (Select None). . . . . . . Cmd+D
Inverse . . . . Cmd+Shift+I
Convert to Image. . . . Cmd+Opt+Shift+Z
Superselect . . . . Cmd+Up
Subselect. . . . . Cmd+Down

View Menu (Mac)

Show All . . . . Cmd+Shift+M
Hide Selection . . . . Cmd+M
Hide Edges . . . . Cmd+H
Full Display/Draft Toggle . . . . . Cmd+K
Fit Selection . . . . Cmd+0 (zero)
100% Magnification. . . . . Cmd+1
200% Magnification. . . . . Cmd+2
400% Magnification. . . . . Cmd+4
50% Magnification . . . . Cmd+5
800% Magnification. . . . . Cmd+8
3200% Magnification. . . . . . . Cmd+3
6400% Magnification. . . . . . . Cmd+6
Show/Hide Rulers . . . . . . Cmd+Opt+R
Fit All . . . . Cmd+Opt+0 (zero)
Zoom Out . . . . Cmd+-
Zoom In. . . . . Cmd++
Zoom In tool . . . . Cmd+space
Zoom Out. . . . . . Cmd+Opt+space+click

Edit Menu (Mac)

Copy . . . . Cmd+C
Clone. . . . . Cmd+Shift+C
Ungroup. . . . . Cmd+U
Paste . . . . Cmd+V
Cut . . . . Cmd+X
Undo . . . . Cmd+Z
Paste Inside. . . . . Cmd+Shift+V
Crop Selected Image. . . . . . Cmd+Opt+C
Edit Grid dialog . . . . Cmd+Opt+G
Create Empty Image (tool) . Cmd+Opt+Y
Redo . . . . Cmd+Shift+Z
Edit Guides dialog. . . Cmd+Opt+Shift+G
Paste Attributes. . . . . Cmd+Opt+Shift+V

Modify Menu (Mac)

Edit Image Object. . . Cmd+Shift+O [oh]
Edit Background Image . . . . Cmd+E
Bring to Front . . . . Cmd+F
Send to Back . . . . Cmd+B
Group . . . . Cmd+G
Object Properties. . . . . Cmd+I
Join. . . . . Cmd+J
Transform . . . . Cmd+T
Rotate 90° CCW . . . . Cmd+7
Rotate 90° CW . . . . Cmd+9
Send Backward. . . . . Cmd+Shift+B
Exit Image Edit Mode . . . . Cmd+Shift+D
Bring Forward . . . . Cmd+Shift+F
Mask Group . . . . Cmd+Shift+G
Split . . . . Cmd+Shift+J
Align Left Edges. . . . . Cmd+Opt+2
Align Vertical Centers . . . . Cmd+Opt+3
Align Right Edges. . . . . . . Cmd+Opt+4
Align Top Edges. . . . . Cmd+Opt+5
Align Horizontal Centers. . . Cmd+Opt+6
Align Objects Bottom . . . . . Cmd+Opt+7
Distribute Widths. . . . . . . Cmd+Opt+8
Distribute Heights . . . . . . Cmd+Opt+9

Text Menu (Mac)

Text Editor . . . . Cmd+Shift+E
Convert to Paths. . . . . Cmd+Shift+P
Attach Text to Path . . . . . . Cmd+Shift+Y
Bold Text . . . . Cmd+Opt+Shift+B
Center-Align Text . . . Cmd+Opt+Shift+C
Italic Text . . . . Cmd+Opt+Shift+I
Justify Text . . . . Cmd+Opt+Shift+J
Left-Align Text . . . . . Cmd+Opt+Shift+L

BoldItalic Text . . Cmd+Opt+Shift+O (oh)
Plain Text Style . . . . . Cmd+Opt+Shift+P
Right-Align Text . . . . Cmd+Opt+Shift+R
Stretch-Justify Text . . . Cmd+Opt+Shift+S

Window Menu (Mac)

Brush panel . . . . Cmd+Opt+B
Effect panel . . . . Cmd+Opt+E
Fill panel . . . . Cmd+Opt+F
Frames panel . . . . Cmd+Opt+K
Layers panel . . . . Cmd+Opt+L
Color Mixer panel. . . . . . Cmd+Opt+M
New Window . . . . Cmd+Opt+N
Tool Options panel . . . Cmd+Opt+O (oh)
Info panel. . . . . Cmd+Opt+I
Opacity panel . . . . Cmd+Opt+P
Swatches panel . . . . Cmd+Opt+S
Toolbox. . . . . Cmd+Opt+T
URLs panel . . . . Cmd+Opt+U

Xtras (Mac)

Cmd+Opt+Shift+X . . . . Repeat Xtra

TOOLBOX KEYBOARD SHORTCUTS

The following are the keys that are used to access the different tools in the toolbox (*see page 13*). These keys are pressed without using any modifier keys such as Command or Ctrl. For instance, to choose the Rectangle tool, you would press the letter *R*. If a letter is used for two tools, such as the *B* for Brush and Reshape Brush, it means that pressing the letter again will toggle between the two tools. Shortcuts for Pixel tools such as the Lasso or Rubber Stamp only work in the Image Editing mode.

Toolbox

A, 1 . . . . Subselection pointer

B . . . . Brush

B . . . . Reshape Path

C . . . . Crop

E . . . . Eraser

F . . . . Freeform Reshape

F . . . . Reshape Area

G . . . . Polygon

H . . . . Hand

I . . . . Eyedropper

J . . . . Export Area

K . . . . Paintbucket

K . . . . Paintbucket (Handles)

L . . . . Lasso

L . . . . Lasso (Polylasso)

M . . . . Marquee (Rectangle)

M . . . . Marquee (Ellipse)

N . . . . Line

P . . . . Pen

Q . . . . Transform tools

R . . . . Rectangle

R . . . . Ellipse

S . . . . Rubber Stamp

T . . . . Text

U . . . . Path Scrubber (+)

U . . . . Path Scrubber (-)

V, zero . . . . Pointer

V, zero . . . . Pointer (Pick Behind)

W . . . . Magic Wand

Y . . . . Pencil

Z . . . . Magnify

INDEX

F

M

X

W